EVERYONE HOT POT

EVERYONE HOT POT

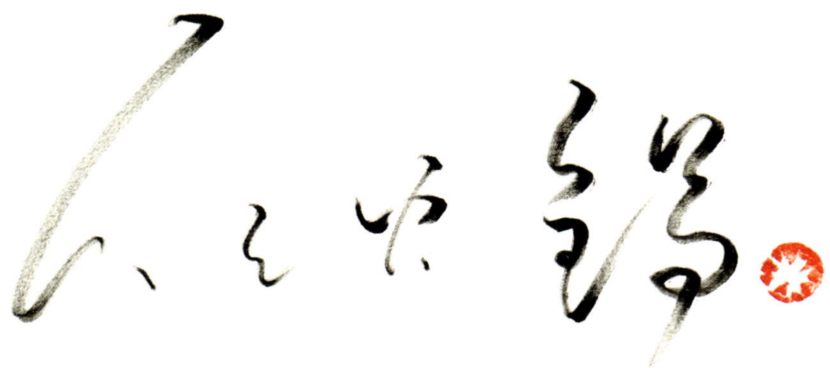

Creating the Ultimate Meal for Gathering and Feasting

NATASHA PICKOWICZ

PHOTOGRAPHS BY ALEX LAU / ILLUSTRATIONS BY LI HUAI

ARTISAN | NEW YORK

Library of Congress Cataloging-in-Publication Data

Names: Pickowicz, Natasha author | Lau, Alex photographer
Title: Everyone hot pot : creating the ultimate meal for gathering and feasting / Natasha Pickowicz ; photographs by Alex Lau.
Description: New York : Artisan, [2026] | Includes index.
Identifiers: LCCN 2025015544 | ISBN 9781648293801 hardback | ISBN 9781648293825 ebook
Subjects: LCSH: Cooking, Asian | One-dish meals—Asia | LCGFT: Cookbooks
Classification: LCC TX724.5.A1 P535 2026 | DDC 641.82095—dc23/eng/20250702
LC record available at https://lccn.loc.gov/2025015544

Design by Nina Simoneaux

Artisan books may be purchased in bulk for business, educational, or promotional use. For information, please contact your local bookseller or the Hachette Book Group Special Markets Department at special.markets@hbgusa.com.

The publisher is not responsible for websites (or their content) that are not owned by the publisher.

The Hachette Speakers Bureau provides a wide range of authors for speaking events. To find out more, go to hachettespeakersbureau.com or email HachetteSpeakers@hbgusa.com.

Published by Artisan,
an imprint of Workman Publishing,
a division of Hachette Book Group, Inc.
1290 Avenue of the Americas
New York, NY 10104
artisanbooks.com

Printed in Malaysia (IVIV) on responsibly sourced paper

First printing, December 2025

1 3 5 7 9 10 8 6 4 2

FOR MY PARENTS

財

—SEAMUS HEANEY

CONTENTS

HAND SANITIZER

INTRODUCTION

"Eat and drink, man and woman—the greatest human desires reside in them."

—FROM *RECORD OF RITES* (*LI JI*), CONFUCIUS

Growing up in San Diego, I counted down the days for summer to end, not begin. The cooler months took their sweet time to roll around, and I longed for "real" weather, which, in the temperate climate of San Diego, meant anything slightly dramatic and uncomfortable. The closest we'd get to that in La Jolla was the thick, wet fog that crawled toward the coast most mornings, or the damp, long nights that left our front lawn sticky with dew.

When fall weather finally approached, there was one certainty in our home: It was time for hot pot. Hot pot is the ancient East Asian cookery method of rapidly poaching bite-size morsels of fresh vegetables, meats, seafood, and tofu in a communal tableside broth. It's the strongest tradition we have in our family; my love for it grows exponentially every year, as I introduce new people to it. The love expands, the circle widens, the tradition shifts.

My mother, Li Huai, an artist born in Beijing, and my father, Paul Pickowicz, a New England–born historian of China, fed me with their homey Chinese cooking. When I was a child, my mom made almost all of our meals, preparing simple, delicious things like soy sauce–braised chicken drumsticks and lap cheong fried rice; soft lobes of tomato folded into scrambled eggs; whole steamed sea bass, stuffed with scallions and glossy with black bean sauce. But it was hot pot that I loved the most, above all others, because it meant that a party was just around the corner. For an only child, the anticipation of joining my parents and their friends at the hot pot table was a thrilling prospect. If other kids were present, we'd clamor

for the best spots at the long dining room table, hoping for a seat inches from a simmering pot perched over the exposed flickering flame of a small camping stove. Endless platters would stretch before me: woven bundles of translucent noodles; frilly clusters of mushrooms and cabbage; tissue-thin slices of raw lamb, pork, and beef; plus my personal dipping bowl, painted with creamy, nutty white sesame sauce, as thick as a smoothie.

As the hours went by and the laughter grew louder, the windows would fog over with the billowing, aromatic steam, like we were in our own heaven, floating away on a cloud we had created. I was free to "play" with my food—fishing for a fallen dumpling or tofu cube with my woven mesh basket, like a competitive game—and I made a mess without chiding or consequence.

These days, when I travel to San Diego to visit my parents, hot pot is the one meal I beg them to reprise, hoping they'll set up their antique copper hot pot, its burnished sides stamped with grimacing lions. Except now, I'm a professional chef, and I insist on making the broth with roasted bones, aromatics, and toasted spices. I visit the farmers' market for greens like chickweed and amaranth to nestle alongside baskets of my mom's store-bought napa cabbage and pea shoots. I add thick coins of creamy, starchy vegetables like purple potatoes and Hakurei turnips to make the broth rich and sweet.

My love for and approach to hot pot have grown and deepened as the years go by. Today, it's evolved into something altogether mine. I feel much less concerned with having hot pot be traditionally "Chinese" than I do with being resourceful and creative with the ingredients available to me. For friends, I'll host relaxed, chatty hot pot parties where there are no rules, no set courses, and barely any prep or cooking to do beforehand (turns out, my friends are happy with frozen scallion pancakes and a bottle of Hennessy). I've converted soup skeptics into hot pot fanatics. I've romanced boyfriends with an intimate hot pot for two (a little sliced steak and scallops go a long way). Like my parents, I hold no greater pride than in sharing hot pot with someone who has never experienced its magic. Somehow, this ancient cookery feels like it belongs to everybody.

My life has been shaped by my love of bringing people together, and hot pot is the ultimate manifestation of this desire. By hosting and sharing, we create moments that are bigger than ourselves, bigger than a single ingredient or dish or tool. It's true: Something ineffable happens over *every* hot pot. People leave relaxed and loose, their eyes heavy and belts tight. My dad always says that at the hot pot table, you could sit next to a stranger, and by the end of the night they'd be your best friend. Now, more than ever, we need these moments to bring us together. Hot pot is the way to do it.

Hot Pot Origins

The Mandarin Chinese phrase for hot pot is *huoguo*, which literally translates to "fire pot." Also called steamboat, or Mongolian pot, hot pot has flourished in China for thousands of years, dating as far back as the Shang and Zhou dynasties (approximately 1600–256 BCE). The more modern version of the hot pot we know today—a communal meal gathered around a metal pot bubbling over a shared heat source—dates as far back as the Three Kingdoms period (280–220 BCE).

During the Yuan dynasty (1279–1368)—the first foreign-ruled dynasty in Chinese history—the Mongols cultivated their own hot pot culture, using the meat of large grazing mammals, such as beef and lamb, as the cornerstone of the meal. Today, we can trace its influence still to the northern and northeastern regions of China, like Beijing, where at-home hot pot tends to be streamlined and basic, with mutton and sliced cabbage forming the base of the communal broth. During the bitterly cold winter season, hot pot both fed the belly and warmed the home. Lacto-fermented vegetables—like cabbage, chives, and radish—added a crucially sharp, piquant balance.

Following the collapse of the Mongol-led Yuan dynasty, hot pot continued to gain in popularity, first during the Ming dynasty (1368–1644), which forwent the Mongolian style of food for flavors from southern China and emphasized vegetables and grains more than meat. During the Manchu-led Qing dynasty (1644–1912), the last imperial dynasty in Chinese history, chefs continued to expand hot pot's cultural practices, incorporating it into lavish palace feasts.

The most famous style of hot pot has its humble origins in Sichuan province of southwestern China, a vast area that stretches out along the Yangtze and Jialing Rivers. Boatmen would paddle up and down the waters, using hot pot as a cost-friendly way to dine while on the go. Today, we associate this style of hot pot with the metropolis of Chongqing (which was part of Sichuan province until 1997 and still, to this day, bears great symbolic association to the region's foodways), where a mouth-numbing, beef-rich, scarlet red broth, spiked with Sichuan peppercorns, chile peppers, and fermented soybeans, is enjoyed year-round, from the damp winters to the deliriously hot summers.

Today hot pot appears in infinite variations throughout China, from the seafood-rich Cantonese style of Guangdong in the south to the mushroomy Yunnan styles in the mountainous regions in the southwest to the chrysanthemum broths of Jiangsu, a coastal province north of Shanghai. In Dongbei, a region in the far northeastern corner of China, a distinctive hot pot style, combining Manchurian, Mongolian, Korean, Russian, and Japanese culinary influences, incorporates beef, corn, squash, green beans, and steamed bread. Truly, there are as many variations to hot pot as there are to soup itself.

Indeed, throughout Asia, endless variations of hot pot appear in all cornerstones of culture and community. In Korea, you'll find jeongol and budae jjigae. In Japan, nabemono encapsulates a whole style of hot pot cooking, including motsunabe and the ever-popular shabu-shabu. Cambodian hot pot, called yao hon, uses coconut milk in the soup base. Thai hot pot, or Thai suki, incorporates lemongrass to perfume the broth. Vietnamese hot pot, called lẩu, harnesses the classic flavors of Viet cooking, like makrut leaves and red chiles.

Hot pot is a cuisine with both high and low origins. For families living in poverty or working-class tradesmen or fishermen, a watery broth enriched with cheap vegetables and tofu was an economical way to stretch a small ration of lamb or beef. For wealthier families and imperial elites, it was a way to signal abundance and splendor, with lavish banquets studded with expensive shellfish, tender meats, and intricate dumplings. These days, hot pot still embodies the entire human experience, from affordable, all-you-can-eat buffets for busy students to annual Lunar New Year reunion feasts for families, where the gathering around the stove (or weilu) is an auspicious symbol of family reunion.

No matter where you are in the world, there are some universal truths to hot pot. It is a uniquely communal act—your guests aren't just diners, but active participants in the feast that unfolds. It takes all the pressure off you, the chef and the host, to perform some elaborate culinary dance. The full scope of the dinner emerges, minute by minute, as the guests cook their bites themselves. It's a millennia-old tradition that is both entertainment *and* nourishment, all rolled into one meal.

How to Use This Book

Hot pot, by its very nature, is the ultimate customizable and modular experience. Prefer to skip meat? The vegan options are endless (see page 157). No time to simmer broth bones for hours? There are pantry solutions for that (Hot Pot Bouillon, page 48). Don't like fish balls? There are plenty of other oceanic treats from which to choose (see page 105). Hosting in the summer? Hot pot is not just for the cold months (see page 187)!

But more to the point, your hot pot is not bound to any strict tradition, set of ingredients, rules, or doctrine. Though it's worth understanding the complex and expansive traditions found all over Asia (and, truly, all over the world), hot pot is an exquisitely intractable thing: It's *not* a rigid, immutable idea but rather a fluid, inclusive philosophy informed by a community's need and shaped by culture and tradition. And as a biracial, California-born chef who has long suffered from feelings of inadequacy and exclusion from mainstream Chinese cultural narratives, coming to this realization was incredibly liberating. Hot pot can be anything I want it to be.

The more I consider what hot pot means to me, the more I realize that I love it not because the meal strictly adheres to any "rules" but because it is an incredibly forgiving and holistic framework for me to bring in other dishes, ingredients, cultures, and aesthetics. Hot pot is not about a monolithic Chinese experience—it generously makes room for you.

A half-empty jar of English marmalade, a bottle of Japanese sake, and a big leafy bunch of Swiss chard from the farmers' market are all equally welcome at my hot pot table—and you *won't* find these idiosyncratic additions at traditional hot pot restaurants. The truth is, no one will be as receptive or as tuned in to your desires as *you* are. No one knows what your family and friends crave for dinner more than you! This is where hot pot gets fun, intimate, creative—and all yours.

As you build your hot pot pantry, sample new ingredients, and set the table, you'll find many opportunities to make this meal your own. You'll find a concise guide to the essential hot pot equipment and tools (see page 18), a sample run of show (see page 40), plus a detailed (but by no means comprehensive!) guide to ingredients (see page 27). You'll discover your new favorite dipping sauce (see page 116)—or just build your own DIY sauce buffet (see page 128), inspired by how the restaurants do it. You'll cherry-pick your favorite cold appetizers (see page 132), hand-shaped breads and dumplings (see page 79), not-too-sweet desserts (see page 162), and soothing drinks (see page 194) to accent your hot pot spread.

To jump-start your own creative juices, I've provided the plans for four showstopping hot pot feasts, each with its own unique theme and point of view. You'll find them peppered throughout, alongside recommendations from one of my favorite wine professionals (see page 206), tips from a self-proclaimed "fruit sommelier" (see page 184), and a cocktail historian's twist on an ancient Chinese spirit (see page 211).

Depending on where you live, you may only be familiar with hot pot as a dining-out option. Whether it's an all-you-can-eat bacchanal or a sleek iPad-operated chain restaurant, you can rely on plenty of theatrics, over-the-top presentation, and bells and whistles. But for many first-generation Asian Americans, like myself, hot pot is a cozy tradition best enjoyed at home, with loved ones. It's time to bring that magic into your home—any way you desire. Everyone, hot pot!

THE HOT POT ESSENTIALS: GETTING STARTED

Hot pot—like a birthday cake, lobster boil, or backyard barbecue—is a phrase that symbolizes so much more than its literal meaning. If you invite someone over for hot pot, the hint has been dropped: Tonight we party, the food is yours to discover, and the person bumping elbows with you is your new best friend. It's as much of a social gathering as it is a meal—you simply don't eat hot pot alone.

Hot pot is easy to pull off for cooks at any skill level—all you need are a few leafy vegetables; a bright, punchy herb; a noodle or dipping bread; and some kind of protein, like shrimp or tofu or thinly sliced meats; coupled with a few indispensable recipes, like a crunchy, cooling salad and a thick, salty dipping sauce.

The most joyful part of prep, for me, comes with setting the table: arranging the ingredients artfully, nudging as many chairs and benches as can fit around the table, selecting the music and flowers and snacks—in other words, getting the atmosphere just right.

Here you'll find everything you need to build a solid foundation to enjoy hot pot. There are guides for the perfect hot pot equipment setup (see page 18), a sample hot pot party run of show (see page 40), and some cheeky hot pot etiquette (see page 119). We'll get to the recipes—but first, you need to shop!

The Equipment: Everything You Need to Set Up for Hot Pot

Most basic hot pot setups can be divided into two parts: a wide, medium-shallow vessel to hold the broth and food, and underneath, a steady source of heat to keep it bubbling away. But there are many updated permutations to this concept that are well suited to the modern home. These days, it's common to find an all-in-one hot pot that has a heating element built right into the cookware—just plug and play. More elaborate gear can incorporate a communal flat-top grill, or plancha element, as well—a beguiling option to sear that bite of food instead. Pick the right one for you!

THE POT

You simply can't enjoy hot pot without a sturdy vessel to contain the simmering soup, and everything from the size, depth, and shape to the material of the pot will contribute to your enjoyment of the meal.

Cooking Pot: If you already have a Dutch oven, soup pot, or stockpot, you're in luck—these items work great for a hot pot. Look for a pot that holds at least 2 to 4 quarts (1.9 to 3.8 L) of liquid, depending on the size of the party, with sides steep enough to contain a bubbling broth but not so tall that it becomes awkward to fish food out of it. Four inches (10 cm) tall is a good rule of thumb.

If you're using an induction burner underneath, be mindful of the material of the pot as well. While cast iron, enameled cast iron, and most forms of stainless steel are induction compatible, aluminum, copper, glass, and ceramic will not work. Avoid any nonstick finishes, which are easily scratched.

PAIR IT WITH: A butane camping stove or electric induction burner.

WHERE TO FIND IT: Online and in kitchen supply stores (see Resources, page 214).

Dual-Chambered Hot Pot: Typically made with thin stainless steel, the "double flavor" or yuan yang hot pot contains a dividing barrier running down the middle, to allow for two distinctly flavored broths, and a tight-fitting, tempered glass lid. Sometimes the barrier undulates, resembling the Tai Chi yin-yang symbol, and this duality can be reflected in the contents of the pot, like one mild and one spicy broth.

PAIR IT WITH: A butane camping stove; these types of pots don't always work on induction burners.

WHERE TO FIND IT: Online and in major Asian grocery stores (see Resources, page 214).

Chimney Hot Pot: This type of container is characteristic of the Beijing-style pot, which is traditionally made with copper or more intricate cloisonné, an ornamental metalwork-decorating technique. The basin is doughnut-shaped, and a tall chimney, fed with smoldering charcoal, pushes through it, heating the water from both the bottom and the center.

> PAIR IT WITH: As the heating element is built right in, all you need are charcoal briquettes or Sterno fuel.
>
> WHERE TO FIND IT: eBay, Etsy, and antique shops (see Resources, page 214).

Nine-Chamber Hot Pot: The "Nine Palaces" hot pot, or jiugongge, from the Chongqing region, is scored into nine small chambers, like the grid of a tic-tac-toe puzzle. Each cube can hold a different broth, at a varying level of spice, intensity, and richness, for Sichuan-style feasts (see page 187).

> PAIR IT WITH: A butane camping stove.
>
> WHERE TO FIND IT: Online and in specialty cookware shops (see Resources, page 214).

Electric Hot Pot: These compact, versatile pots have an electric heat source built right in, and they offer a great deal of variety in design, color, and size. They tend to be more expensive and come with timers and dials for adjusting temperature and more. At least 1,300 watts will keep the broth at a rolling boil.

> PAIR IT WITH: A nearby electrical outlet.
>
> WHERE TO FIND IT: Look for brands like Dezin, TopWit, and Zojirushi online or in major Asian grocery and kitchen supply stores (see Resources, page 214).

HEAT SOURCES

You'll be cooking your food right at the table, which poses a unique challenge: finding a heat source that can be easily controlled, contained, and safe. Most hot pot restaurants engineer custom tabletops with the heating element built right in, but at home, you have two options with which to create the perfect movable feast.

Induction Cooktop: These burners require an electrical outlet to function and use magnetic waves to rapidly heat cookware to a temperature that you can control through digital buttons or dials. Induction cooktops are the safest and most environmentally friendly of all the heat source options, but they can vary in quality and get expensive. (Be sure to tape down any running cables on the floor to prevent tripping!) Look for at least 1,600 watts and a glass surface.

WHERE TO FIND IT: Online and in kitchen supply and hardware stores (see Resources, page 214).

Butane Camping Stove: These stoves, fed by canisters of butane gas, are cheap, portable, easy to use, and compatible with just about every kind of cooking vessel out there. They come with levers to click the gas into place, spark the pilot, and adjust the intensity of the flame. A cartridge of gas, at high power, will last about 90 minutes. Butane canisters are usually sold in packs of four and should be stored safely and away from heat. Iwatani makes beautiful models (see Resources, page 214), but utilitarian versions can be found for less than $20. Most come in compact carrying cases to make storage and transport easy.

WHERE TO FIND IT: Online and in Asian supermarkets and hardware stores (see Resources, page 214).

ESSENTIAL TOOLS

You'll need these handy tools to assist you in the endless transfer from the platter to the hot pot to your mouth. For a list of some of my favorite retailers, visit Resources (page 214).

For Each Person

Chopsticks: Personal chopsticks are for consuming everything from a tangle of noodles to slippery greens; it's nice to offer forks in case that is a diner's preferred utensil.

Chopstick Rest: There are plenty of objects around your home that could work as a chopstick rest—get creative! My mom likes small, smooth stones; I love decorative, edible items from the farmers' market, like purple okra, a flat potato, or a baby carrot.

Hot Pot Strainer: Whether made with fine mesh or a coarser woven wire, a hot pot strainer (sometimes labeled as a scoop, spider, or skimmer) provides guests with a hands-off method of containing bites that have a longer cook time, like starchy vegetables, small clams, and dumplings. The long handle can (and should!) be bent in half to hook against the side of the hot pot vessel. Larger straining vessels, like deep cylinders or baskets made with fine mesh meant for deep-frying, best control slippery, hard-to-manage ingredients, like glass noodles.

Napkins: Hot pot can get messy! For an added layer of protection, you can offer a small lobster bib to protect any cute outfits from soup splatters.

Shot Glass: It's not hot pot without shots! If you don't have baijiu, a strong Chinese whiskey typically served in a small glass, it's nice to shoot *something*, even if it's just beer or fizzy water.

Small Side Plate: A side plate (like a bread plate about 5 to 6 inches/12 to 15 cm across) holds cooked ingredient overflow and is handy for stashing flaky breads, cold appetizers, and anything you don't immediately want to dunk in the dipping sauce.

Small Soup Bowl: A small soup bowl (about 4 inches/10 cm across) can house each person's dipping sauce.

Soup Spoon: An Asian soup spoon is best for slurping hot soup and cradling big, juicy bites, like dumplings.

Water Glass or Ceramic Tea Cup: Even if you plan on serving fancier beverages, like a fresh fruit juice or fizzy wine, make sure your guests are staying hydrated by providing plenty of water or hot tea.

For the Table

The hot pot table is a dizzying mix of ingredients, both raw and cooked. Choosing the right utensils and servingware—and assigning them a specific purpose—helps organize the spread and assist your guests. For table design inspiration, read about the favorite independent designers and retailers used by Kalen Kaminski, the artist and prop stylist behind every photograph here (see Resources, page 214).

Oversize Chopsticks, Tongs, or Serving Forks: Though it's perfectly acceptable to transfer some ingredients from the platter to the hot pot with clean hands (like leafy vegetables, herbs, or noodles), juicier items require utensils. Designate a pair of oversize chopsticks or tongs for thinly sliced seafood and meat and a pair of tongs for handling unwieldy, chunkier items. It's proper food safety practice to not cross-contaminate utensils or to eat using any of the shared tools.

Soup Ladle: Perfect for portioning broth into your small soup bowl, a ladle can be shared by everyone throughout the night.

Servingware: At hot pot restaurants, where patrons order ingredients à la carte, the dishes come out individually on small plates. At home, however, this arrangement may be less realistic to execute, and you'll want to use larger pieces, like platters and salad bowls, to cluster all your favorite ingredients. Shallow bowls are best for nestling fragile ingredients, like bundles of noodles or tender sprouts. Flat plates are best for showcasing thin curls of meat. For plating ideas, see The Decor (page 43).

Hot Pot: The Ultimate Feast on a Budget

HOT POT IS A SHOWY, impressive meal—but that doesn't mean you have to break the bank to do it. You probably already own most of the tools to enjoy hot pot, so don't feel pressured to buy everything recommended here. Plunder your cutlery drawer for forks, spoons, tongs, and ladles; start stockpiling disposable chopsticks from your favorite Asian takeout. A bounty of photogenic ingredients will make even the most mismatched place settings and platters look chic, but for sets of sturdy plates, turn to restaurant and kitchen supply stores and warehouses, which offer better prices for larger quantities of items like small plates, small bowls, shot glasses, and more. If you don't have a tableside heating element, you will need to buy one—go for a basic camping stove and you'll spend $20. You'll be able to repurpose it for all of your alfresco meals, like Korean barbecue or fondue. And don't forget—Asian families love to share. In planning my more ambitious hot pots, I've borrowed from friends everything from burners to extra chairs to platters to teapots.

The Spread: Everything to Know About Everything to Eat

When it comes to what goes into your bubbling hot pot broth, there's basically no limit to what you can include. And if you're like me, a trip to the grocery store can get overwhelming—there are just so many tempting decisions to make, and it can be hard to know how much food is "enough" for a hungry group of two, four, or twelve.

While you can certainly produce a legitimate hot pot experience with just a handful of simpatico ingredients, the delirious fun of it all is to overload the senses with a colorful, abundant, surprising table of items that draw on different textures, flavors, and sensations. After all, the best part of any hot pot feast is debating your favorite bites!

It's essential to write a shopping list while also remaining open-minded and willing to improvise. From a solid list, you can (and should!) go off course, curating the offerings based on your palate and budget. Love fungi? Pick two or three different mushrooms. Craving leafy greens? My mom will approve if you feature more than three. There are no wrong answers!

To get the most out of your hot pot experience, keep your eyes peeled for even more organizational tips from Tyna Hoang, the food stylist behind some of my favorite cookbooks (and this one, too).

Everything you choose will be cooked in a flavorful broth (see page 47), and you'll supplement those ingredients with a vivid dipping sauce (see page 116). For the full experience, don't forget a chilled appetizer (see page 132), a refreshing drink (see page 194), and a light dessert (see page 162)!

I've curated four themed hot pot menus that conjure a wide range of hot pot experiences, from a summery vegan feast (see page 157) to a fiery Sichuan-inspired banquet (see page 187). If you'd like to go that route, the full plan is mapped out for you.

As far as the quantities of each ingredient, I tend to overpurchase—after all, you're buying raw ingredients that can easily be packed up at the end of the night and used for cooking throughout the week. You'll need about 28 ounces (790 g) of food and 1 quart (950 ml) of broth for each guest. (That 28 ounces of food per guest accounts for 1 pound/450 g of vegetables, 6 ounces/170 g of starches, and 6 ounces/170 g of protein.) Generally speaking, for a typical hot pot party of four, you will need:

4 quarts (3.8 L) broth (or 2 quarts/1.9 L each of two broths)
4 pounds (1.8 kg) mixed vegetables and herbs
1½ pounds (680 g) dumplings, noodles, or breads
1½ pounds (680 g) meat, seafood, or tofu

YOUR HOT POT SPREAD EQUATION

1 leafy green + 1 fresh herb + 1 bite-size protein + 1 hearty starch
= your dream hot pot

PROCESSING YOUR HOT POT HAUL: FOR EVERY CUT THERE IS A REASON

Once the shopping is complete, all that's left to do is clean and process your ingredients—no advance cooking required. The most important thing to remember is that *all* of the food should be bite-size: Each morsel should be small enough to nestle into a personal mesh basket, pick up with chopsticks, and fit in your mouth.

The best hot pot morsels prioritize expediency: The smaller the piece of food, the more quickly it will cook, and the less unwieldy it will be to eat. This is not the time for a long braise, so varying bites should occur in rapid succession. Everything should cook in a matter of seconds or minutes, and in the case of ingredients that traditionally need more time (such as squash or potatoes), an intentional knife cut is essential to coaxing out tenderness.

Meat is presented in translucent slices, sometimes rolled into tidy cigars, which are easy for chopsticks to handle. Paper-thin slices have the added bonus of tenderizing cuts that need hours to cook, like beef short ribs or pork belly. Seafood stays succulent with a quick dip in the broth, but, like meat, most seafood will get tough and chewy if it boils for too long or is forgotten.

THE HOT POT INGREDIENT GUIDE: WHAT TO BUY, HOW TO PREP, AND COOKING TIMES

These ingredients make up the core of hot pot; a speedy dip into a hot broth is all it takes to achieve success. Follow the foolproof Spread Equation (previous page) for a well-balanced buffet that guarantees something delicious for everyone at the table.

Finally, ingredients come in all states: fresh, dried, cured, fried, frozen, and more. The freezer aisle is a terrific place to stock up on hot pot essentials, from fish balls to dumplings to thinly sliced meats, so don't skip it.

When preparing your hot pot ingredients, the most important rule to remember is that every piece of food should be bite-size—not too small, not too big, but just right. You can (and should) have fun and experiment with your knife cuts—some days call for bean curd cubes, other days require bean curd slabs—as long as you stay mindful of the overall surface area. That's the fun of hot pot—a never-ending sequence of small mouthfuls of food eventually add up to one seriously nourishing meal.

Fresh and Fragrant Herbs

You'll smell them before you see them—fresh herbs are essential for bringing intense flavor and brightness to any bite.

Shop: Scallions, chives, yellow chives, cilantro, basil, Thai basil, mint, parsley, perilla, shiso.

Prep: Wash well and pat dry. Scallions and chives can be portioned into 2-inch (5 cm) batons. Leafy herbs can be kept whole. Transfer to a bowl or plate and cover with a wet towel.

TYNA'S TIP

Wrap herbs loosely in a damp paper towel, then place them in a sealed ziplock bag, and store them in the crisper drawer in your fridge—they'll last for weeks that way.

Cook: The herbs can be added to the broth to season the soup or briefly dunked in broth before being consumed with heartier ingredients.

Delicate Sprouts, Shoots, and Microgreens

Cheap, bountiful, and with a fresh, sweet, and sometimes spicy crunch, sprouts add texture and lightness to heavier bites. Mung bean sprouts are so flavorful and nutty that they're often used for making stock, too.

Shop: Radish sprouts, mung bean sprouts, watercress, nasturtium, snow pea shoots, amaranth.

Prep: Wash well and pat dry. Transfer to a deep bowl and cover with a damp towel.

Cook: These ingredients can be eaten raw, as a refreshing, crunchy foil, or poached quickly in the broth for about 15 seconds.

Tender Leafy Greens

These greens aren't just for salad—a quick dunk in hot broth adds a nutrient-charged jolt to your feast.

Shop: Spinach, romaine lettuce, Little Gem lettuce, chrysanthemum greens, sweet potato leaves, sorrel, turnip greens, beet tops.

Prep: Wash well and pat dry. If the greens are connected as a bunch, tear them apart into small, bite-size clusters.

Cook: For a quick blanch with some lingering crispness, use your chopsticks to plunge a bite of greens in and out of the broth. For a softer cook, simmer in a basket for 5 to 10 seconds.

Firmer Leafy Greens

These veggies are more fibrous and can be steamed, braised, or boiled for longer periods of time. Their versatility shines in hot pot: A quick blanch retains structure and crunch, while a longer cook transforms them into silky, melt-in-your-mouth ribbons.

Shop: Collard greens, mustard greens, kale, Swiss chard, leeks.

Prep: Wash well and pat dry. Strip the greens of their tough inner ribs, if they have them. Tear the leaves into large pieces and roll up into cigars or layer into a bowl.

Cook: For crunchy greens, blanch for just a minute. For softer greens, boil for at least 4 to 5 minutes.

Chunky, Crunchy Vegetables

Brassicas and root vegetables turn sweet, nutty, and creamy in the hot pot. The tiny florets of cruciferous vegetables are like sponges; they soak up intense broth and sauces.

Shop: Celtuce, broccoli, broccolini, sprouting cauliflower, gai lan (Chinese broccoli), Hakurei turnips, kohlrabi, long beans, daikon radish, taro, lotus root.

Prep: Wash well and pat dry. Chop larger heads into smaller, bite-size florets. Gai lan, turnips, and long beans stay whole; radish, kohlrabi, and celtuce should be peeled and diced into 1-inch (2.5 cm) cubes or sliced on the bias into 2-inch (5 cm) planks.

Cook: For an al dente crunch, small florets and pieces should be blanched for no longer than 1 minute. For a softer mouthfeel, aim for up to 4 minutes.

Frilly, Full Cabbages

A true workhorse of the hot pot table, these brassicas are cheap, ubiquitous, and a marvel of texture. Napa cabbage is the standard choice, but many farmers' markets offer smaller heads of tender, thin-leaved cabbages, like the cone-shaped Caraflex and flat Saku Saku.

Shop: Purple cabbage, napa cabbage, green cabbage, savoy cabbage, Saku Saku cabbage, Caraflex cabbage, bok choy, yu choy.

Prep: Wash well and pat dry. Long and narrow cabbages, like napa or Caraflex, can be sliced into quarters or eighths, tip to stem. Slice out the core at an angle to make individual long pieces, and cut them in half crosswise for bite-size portions. Round heads of cabbage can be cut into squares or a thin ribbon shred. Bite-size greens, like bok choy, can be left whole or cut in half lengthwise.

Cook: Napa cabbage and bok choy are more tender and cook quickly, about 1 minute per piece. Tougher cabbage needs a slightly longer braise; aim for 3 to 4 minutes for al dente. Supersoft, tender cabbage is also delicious—it's a vegetable you can "forget" about and enjoy with soup at the very end of the meal.

Starchy, Soft Gourds and the Like

Though they take longer to cook, starchy, creamy vegetables add so much body and balance to hot pot. Experiment with knife cuts, like thin potato chip–ish slices, chunky cross-sections, and bite-size cubes.

Shop: Pumpkin, kabocha squash, acorn squash, sweet potato, yams, corn on the cob, fingerling potatoes, carrots.

Prep: Wash well and pat dry. Peel the vegetable if the outer rind isn't edible (like with pumpkin). Slice sweet potato, acorn squash, yams, and carrots into ⅓-inch-thick (1 cm) coins. Gourds can be cubed into 1-inch (2.5 cm) pieces or sliced into ¼-inch-thick (0.6 cm) wedges. Corn on the cob can be chopped into 2-inch (5 cm) cross-sections (you'll eat the kernels right off the cob).

Cook: For a soft, creamy mouthfeel, blanch each piece for 2 to 3 minutes. You can check for doneness by holding the morsel in a wire basket and gently nudging it with a chopstick. The flesh should immediately crumble and split when poked.

CHUNKY, CRUNCHY VEGETABLES

FRILLY, FULL CABBAGES

STARCHY, SOFT GOURDS AND THE LIKE

HOT (POT) TIPS

Taro and potatoes can add a cloudiness and dusty mouthfeel to a delicate broth. To remove some of their starches, store your prepped cubes or slices in cold water for at least 30 minutes before draining and serving at the table.

Hot pot is a group activity, and it takes a village. If you notice a forgotten bite bobbing around the hot pot—and it's completely understandable to lose track of it all, given the frenetic activity and free-flowing drinks—you are empowered to rescue it from the broth, dropping it into a neighbor's bowl (or take it for yourself).

Mushrooms

What *don't* mushrooms improve? Enoki and beech mushrooms are an especially popular hot pot ingredient—their spongy stems and caps eagerly soak up liquid and thick sauces.

Shop: King trumpet, oyster, maitake, enoki, beech, white button, shiitake, lion's mane, wood ear, cremini, portobello, matsutake—you're limited only by your grocery store selection (and wallet).

Prep: Wash well and pat dry. Large mushrooms can be sliced into ⅓-inch-thick (1 cm) slabs. Small mushrooms that grow in tight clusters can be gently pried apart with your fingertips to form bite-size pieces.

Cook: Chewier mushrooms like shiitake need around 4 minutes to become tender; frillier mushrooms like maitake need just a minute or two.

Bonus! Broth Builders

These ingredients can be added to the broth intermittently to provide a boost of flavor to the hot pot, especially if you're just starting with a plain water base. Visually, a raft of chiles or flowers floating on the surface sets an enchanting mood.

Shop: Dried chrysanthemum tea, sliced fresh ginger, peeled garlic cloves, fresh lemongrass, dried jujubes, dried goji berries, dried longan, dried mandarin peel, dried chile peppers, dried shrimp, dried scallops, dried flounder.

Prep: Before you start adding other ingredients, simply open the bag and scatter 1 to 2 tablespoons of each desired ingredient over the broth.

Cook: Cook for as long as you want.

Thinly Sliced Meat

This isn't the time for large chunky cuts of meat. At the grocery store, look for meat (both fresh and frozen) sliced very thinly, either stacked into flat layers or rolled up into batons. Many Asian grocery stores note the actual width of the meat on the label: 1.5 to 2 mm thickness is best; avoid thicker cuts, which can go up to 10 mm, as they're best for other preparations, like Korean barbecue.

Offal, or organ meat, is a very popular hot pot addition. Tripe, heart, blood, brain, liver, kidneys, gizzard, you name it—all add an extra layer of richness and texture to the offerings. They should also be sliced thinly or portioned into bite-size pieces before being presented at the hot pot table.

HOT (POT) TIP

To portion meat yourself, freeze a 6- to 8-ounce (170 to 225 g) piece for 30 minutes, then shave the meat from top to bottom with a cleaver or chef's knife. Slice against the grain of the muscle, which tenderizes the meat.

Shop: Beef top sirloin, rib eye, brisket, chuck, short rib or belly; pork belly, loin, or butt; sliced chicken breast or thigh; lamb shoulder, loin, or leg.

Prep: Thaw any frozen meats before serving, discarding any water that gathers as they defrost. Carefully separate the layers and transfer to a serving plate or baking sheet, fanning them out into a decorative design.

Cook: Because the meat is so thin, it requires little more than heating through. Hold it with your chopsticks or fork and swish it through the simmering broth until it turns opaque, 10 to 15 seconds. More visible fat marbling on the cut of meat (like the belly) means the bite can stand to be cooked longer. Lean cuts of meat (like the loin) are more at risk of being overcooked.

Synchronized Swapping: The Best Ingredient Substitutions

DEPENDING ON WHERE you live, the stores available to you, and your own budget and taste, you might be wondering how to make thoughtful substitutions in your hot pot ingredient sourcing. Fret not—wherever you are, these ingredients remain flexible and will happily bend to meet your own needs and circumstances. While not all ingredients have a clear substitution (sorry, but there's just no replacement for singular ingredients like black vinegar or baijiu), here are some successful one-to-one substitutions for you to consider.

INSTEAD OF . . .		TRY . . .
Asian milk bread	→	Brioche
Bean curd sheets	→	Yuba sheets
Calamansi juice	→	Equal parts lime juice and orange juice
Chinese celery	→	Celery
Chinese white sesame paste	→	Tahini, peanut butter
Dried hawthorn berries	→	Dried cherries
Dried jujubes	→	Dates, dried apples
Dried salted plum	→	Equal parts apricot jam and apple cider vinegar
Fermented black bean sauce	→	Hoisin sauce
Fresh wood ear mushrooms	→	Dried fungus, dried wood ear mushrooms
Gochugaru chile flakes	→	Aleppo chile flakes, espelette pepper flakes
Jicama	→	Radish, apple
Lemongrass	→	Lime juice
Mung beans	→	Canned navy beans, brown lentils
Pea shoots	→	Watercress, romaine lettuce
Shaoxing wine	→	Sherry vinegar
Shiso	→	Perilla, mint, lemon verbena

Seafood

Hot pot is a stellar way to enjoy a variety of fresh or frozen seafood, as you can source smaller quantities of high-end ingredients but still have the table look full and luxurious. Look for a firm, flaky large fish, like branzino, halibut, cod, salmon, or sea bass. Avoid super-delicate fish, like flounder, or smaller bony fish, like mackerel. Fish balls, a processed bite-size treat comprising an emulsified blend of seafood farce, binding starches, and seasoning, are always a hit at hot pot—they're best after 2 minutes in the broth to heat them through.

Shop: Scallops, diver scallops, fish fillets, clams, mussels, shrimp, squid tentacles and calamari rings, sliced abalone, conch, lobster claws, and crab legs.

Prep: Shellfish, well rinsed and scrubbed, should go into the pot unshucked, so their shells can contribute to the flavoring of the broth. Portion fish fillets into 1-inch (2.5 cm) large chunks. Frozen seafood should be fully thawed for the best presentation, but it's not necessary. Shrimp should be shelled and deveined for ease of eating. If you're using crab, lobster, or any crustacean in its shell, be sure to also provide crackers and picks for extracting the meat.

HOT (POT) TIP

Roe, or cured fish eggs, is a delicious and decadent topping for hot pot. Keep roe on the table, its container nestled into ice, so guests can spoon small amounts over cooked seafood, vegetables, rice, and more.

Cook: Clams and mussels boil until the shells swing open, 1 to 2 minutes. Swish fish and shrimp in the simmering broth with chopsticks or perch in a basket until it is just opaque and barely cooked through, 30 seconds to 1 minute; do not overcook, which results in tough, gummy bites. Crab and lobster, in the shell, should be boiled until just cooked through, 5 to 6 minutes.

Noodles

Translucent "glass" noodles, which are typically made with a plant-based starch like mung bean, tapioca, or sweet potato, are the best for hot pot. They are cheap, cook quickly, and have a delightful bounciness. Avoid thick, wheat-based noodles like udon, which get mushy and cloud the broth. But if you'd like to use a floury noodle, like instant ramen or a thin egg noodle, add it at the very end of the hot pot meal.

Shop: Glass noodles or vermicelli (also labeled bean thread noodles, mung bean noodles, or cellophane noodles), rice sticks (sometimes called rice vermicelli), wide sweet potato noodles, kelp or seaweed noodles, instant ramen, pho noodles, egg noodles.

NOODLES

BEAN CURD

MISCELLANEOUS GOODIES

CARB-Y SHORTCUTS

Prep: Dried noodles that are packed into large blocks can be torn apart to form smaller parcels.

Cook: Most thin noodles take several minutes to soften, while wider, chewy noodles made out of ingredients like sweet potato or rice can take much longer; always check the package for suggested cooking instructions. It's traditional to add enough noodles to the pot to feed the entire table, with one person doling out the noodles to all when they're ready.

Bean Curd

The ultimate hot pot shape-shifter, bean curd (or tofu) is made with ground, pressed soybeans and comes in many variations, offering a million choices for flavor, texture, and density.

Shop: For fresh bean curd, look for firm slabs stored in water (silken or soft tofu will disintegrate in the hot pot). For fried bean curd, look for puffs, rolls, cubes, and pockets. Also incredibly popular in hot pot are all types of tofu skins, which are made with the film that forms during the boiling of soy milk. Fresh sheets are called yuba, bean curd sheets, skins or rolls (see page 148). They're also found dehydrated and shelf-stable, often called "dried bean curd"; look for bite-size shapes like knots and sticks. Finally, don't forget the ultra-flavorful slabs of smoked bean curd or fermented or stinky tofu.

Prep: Drain fresh bean curd and slice into 1-inch-wide (2.5 cm) cubes. Sheets of tofu skins can be sliced into linguine-esque noodles.

Cook: Cook fresh and deep-fried bean curd until heated through, about 20 seconds. Pressed sheets and noodles heat through in 1 to 2 minutes. Chewier, denser bites, like dried tofu knots or sticks, can take up to 5 minutes to fully soften.

Miscellaneous Goodies

You're limited only by your appetite and imagination!

Shop: Dried seaweed like hijiki or wakame, kelp knots, quail eggs, Spam, cocktail sausages, cherry tomatoes, kimchi.

Carb-y Shortcuts

If you don't have time to whip up fresh breads, dumplings, or rice, fret not—there's plenty to choose from at the grocery store. Your best bet is the freezer aisle, where you'll be able to survey a wide variety of starches stuffed with innumerable tasty fillings.

HOT (POT) TIP

You tiao, a light, savory deep-fried dough, is often paired with hot pot, and the crisp, golden sticks happily soak up broth. It is sold in the bakery sections, refrigerated cases, and freezer aisles of Asian grocery stores.

Shop: Frozen dumplings (look for classic flavor combinations like scallops and pea shoot; pork and shrimp; or mushroom and cabbage); frozen breads, such as scallion pancakes (cong you bing) or sesame flatbreads (shaobing); frozen doughnuts or crullers (you tiao). You'll also find fresh bread packaged in plastic bags in the refrigerated aisles, near the dairy section, or in the bakeries that sometimes appear at the front of the store.

Cook: Check package instructions; most breads can be reheated in the oven or toaster or fried in a pan. Cook dumplings from frozen; check package for recommended cooking time.

HOT (POT) TIP

Avoid delicate items that are meant to be steamed (like soup dumplings or most dim sum), which would fall apart in the rolling broth.

Building the Perfect Skewer: Adding Flair and Ease with Colorful Bites

MALATANG-STYLE SKEWERS (or chuan-er), a descendant of Chinese Islamic cuisine of the Uyghur people, offer a clever shortcut to enjoying hot pot. If you've ever wandered an outdoor market or food court in a major Chinese city, you might spot vendors offering preassembled skewers of meat and vegetables, built to be plunged into a spicy soup. At home, skewers are a creative way of presenting curated, compatible bites; just remember to group items with similar cooking times. To cook a skewer, baskets or chopsticks are not required—just slip the skewer into the broth, letting it rest against the wall of the hot pot, where it will cook.

These skewers allow you to build flavorful bites through layers of flavor and texture. Look for bamboo skewers at least 6 inches (15 cm) long. Flexible, sheer ingredients, like tofu skins or thin slices of meat, can wrap or envelop pieces with more structure, like mushrooms or scallops. Tucking in herbs or leafy greens adds a boost of flavor and aroma. Prepare the skewers up to a day in advance, keeping them wrapped tightly on a tray in the fridge until your guests arrive.

1 bite-size cluster of enoki mushrooms + 2 slices of Wagyu beef tenderloin

COOK TIME: 1 minute

1 crescent of kabocha squash + 1 sheet of tofu skin

COOK TIME: 2 to 3 minutes

1 tail-attached shrimp + 1 kale leaf

COOK TIME: 1 minute

3 napa cabbage leaves + 3 slices of pork shoulder, alternating

COOK TIME: 2 to 3 minutes

1 king trumpet mushroom slice + 1 scallion green, threaded through

COOK TIME: 2 minutes

2 cubes tofu + 2 cherry tomatoes, alternating

COOK TIME: 2 minutes

4 bay scallops + 1 fava bean, alternating

COOK TIME: 1 minute

The Plan: The Official Run of Show

As the host of a hot pot party, you'll do a lot less actual cooking than you would with other kinds of dinner parties, but it still pays off to plan ahead. When I worked in fine-dining restaurants, whenever there was a big wedding or special event, we'd draw up a preparatory "run of show"—a precise, living document that outlines every hour of the event from start to finish.

Once your guests arrive, give yourself a grace period before diving into hot pot—put out a cold drink and light, salty snacks, or xiao chi (see page 135), which stimulate the appetite for food *and* conversation. Don't worry about enforcing a strict curfew—the magical, meandering nature of the hot pot is determined, in part, by your guests' energy levels, the proclivity for lively conversation, and the spell any alcoholic beverages may cast upon the table. You can't plan everything, nor should you want to.

As the host, you lead by example. Kick things off by demonstrating the basic hot pot choreography: selecting a morsel, wagging it through the flavorful liquid, dunking it in your dipping sauce, and then shoving it right into your mouth. This is not about stockpiling a heaping bowl of cooked food; hot pot is about the endless series of back-and-forth movements of cooking and eating that can, and should, stretch on for hours.

THE DAY BEFORE YOUR HOT POT MEAL

Make room. Empty a shelf in your refrigerator and freezer to create plenty of space for all the ingredients that are about to head your way.

Take inventory. Run through your pantry, noting which spices, sauces, and condiments you have and which ones you'll need to purchase. Get a count of chopsticks and other tools and items (see page 22) for all the guests.

Write a list. Separate your needs into categories: fresh (vegetables, bean curd, fruit, ferments), meats and seafood, frozen (dumplings, breads), pantry (condiments, noodles, spices, dried mushrooms, teas), and snacks (nuts, crackers, and drinks).

Go shopping. A trip to a major Asian grocery store, like H Mart or 99 Ranch Market, is the most efficient strategy—you'll find everything from table settings to butane gas to fresh vegetables to frozen treats. You could also divide your shopping up into smaller specialty trips, with multiple stops to see your favorite butcher, fishmonger, and farmers' market. Order harder-to-find ingredients online—just give yourself enough lead time for packages to arrive promptly (see Resources, page 214).

Make broth. If you're making the broth from scratch (see page 47), beginning it the day before allows the liquid to rest and deepen in flavor.

THE DAY OF YOUR HOT POT MEAL

2 p.m. Mix your sauces (see page 116) and set them aside to rest. If you're making dumplings, prepare them now and put them in the freezer (see page 91).

4 p.m. Wash and dry all the fresh vegetables and fruits. Trim, slice, and chop ingredients before arranging artfully on platters and bowls (see page 43). If you're planning to serve beer and wine, transfer them to your refrigerator, if needed.

5:30 p.m. Set the table (see page 43). Batch out a cocktail or spritz, if making (see page 194).

6 p.m. Your guests are arriving! Reheat the broth in stockpots on the stove and fill a teakettle with water. Present your guests with something cold or fizzy and a few bowls of crunchy snacks.

6:30 p.m. Pan-fry or oven-bake any flaky breads, if using (see page 79), and hold them in a kitchen towel or a barely warm oven.

6:45 p.m. Set out a few cold appetizers (see page 132). Bring out prebuilt platters of vegetables and proteins. Ladle a small amount of dipping sauce into each guest's bowl. Transfer the warm broth to the hot pot topper, adding any fresh herbs or decor to finish.

7 p.m. Invite your guests to sit at the table. Provide a general overview of the spread at hand, pointing out items that have particular cooking times and explaining any unfamiliar or notable ingredients.

7:30 p.m. At regular intervals, invite your guests to make toasts and share a sip of baijiu, if they'd like.

8 p.m. If needed, replenish the table with backup platters of chilled sliced meats and vegetables. Diminishing broth levels should be remedied with boiling hot water from a kettle.

9 p.m. If you sense that hot pot is beginning to wind down and guests are nearing satiation, you have the option of capping the evening with a small bowl of soup, made with the hours-long communally made broth, swirled into the dregs of your dipping sauce bowl. Ladle a small amount of soup into each person's bowl, signaling the end of the hot pot session.

9:30 p.m. Ask everyone to pitch in clearing the table, and boil water for hot tea.

9:45 p.m. If you have the space, you can retreat to a cozier room for more wine, tea, and fresh fruit or a light dessert (see page 162); otherwise, you can stay seated around the table.

10:30 p.m. If you have any leftovers, pack them up into airtight containers and transfer to the refrigerator or freezer. If you like, send your guests home with deli containers stuffed with fresh vegetables, herbs, and noodles—a mini jump start on their grocery shopping and lunch or dinner for the next day.

11:30 p.m. Drink a big glass of water—you'll sleep well tonight.

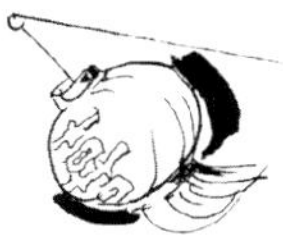

The Decor: Setting the Mood

Because you're not cooking your hot pot ingredients in advance, it's the perfect opportunity to go wild and artful with presentation. Often my most memorable tablescapes come into focus not because I had everything I needed, but because I had to get creative with what I already had. Cutting boards, cake stands, tiered seafood towers, flower vases—are all fair game when it comes to the hot pot table.

Think multipurpose. Have a dual-chambered hot pot topper? It's not just for broth—try serving a duet of cocktails, side by side, in your makeshift punchbowl. Similarly, a Dutch oven filled with ice is a great and unexpected tableside wine and beer bucket.

Add florals to make ingredients pop. Scatter a few edible flowers or herb sprigs over monochromatic plates of meat or seafood.

Go monochromatic. Create dramatic, tonal looks by clustering ingredients of the same color together.

Think vertical. To save space, ingredients can be arranged intentionally, creating structurally sound pyramids that look great. Leafy greens can be arranged in tall vases, standing upright, like an edible bouquet of flowers.

Cake stands aren't just for sweets. Elevated cake stands and tiered seafood towers present a multitude of ingredients without sacrificing precious table surface area. Long, leafy greens can be draped over the edges, like ruffly, cascading curtains, or curled around small dishes containing luxury ingredients.

TYNA'S TIP

A hot pot feast should always be a sight to behold. There are feelings of lust, admiration, and shyness when viewing the table—no one wants to disturb the display. That is what you want to achieve when building a hot pot spread: bounty and drama. I love building height by stacking bricks of tofu cubes into pyramids, fluffing tender greens into tall baskets, and even arranging coils of frozen meat into a dramatic cake!

Pair ingredients with the servingware. Shallow bowls are best for nestling fragile ingredients, like bundles of noodles or tender sprouts. Quarter-sheet baking trays are a great option for presenting raw meats or seafood or anything partially frozen; the inch-high walls of the tray hold in juices as ingredients thaw, and the trays are easy to stack in the fridge.

Go modular. If you'd like to present ingredients on their own, small rectangular or square plates fit snugly on the table, with no wasted surface area.

Keep it cool with ice. Temperature-sensitive ingredients, like sliced fish or meat and raw shellfish and bivalves, can be kept cold if draped over pebbled or crushed ice mounded in a bowl.

BROTHS

The Soul of Hot Pot

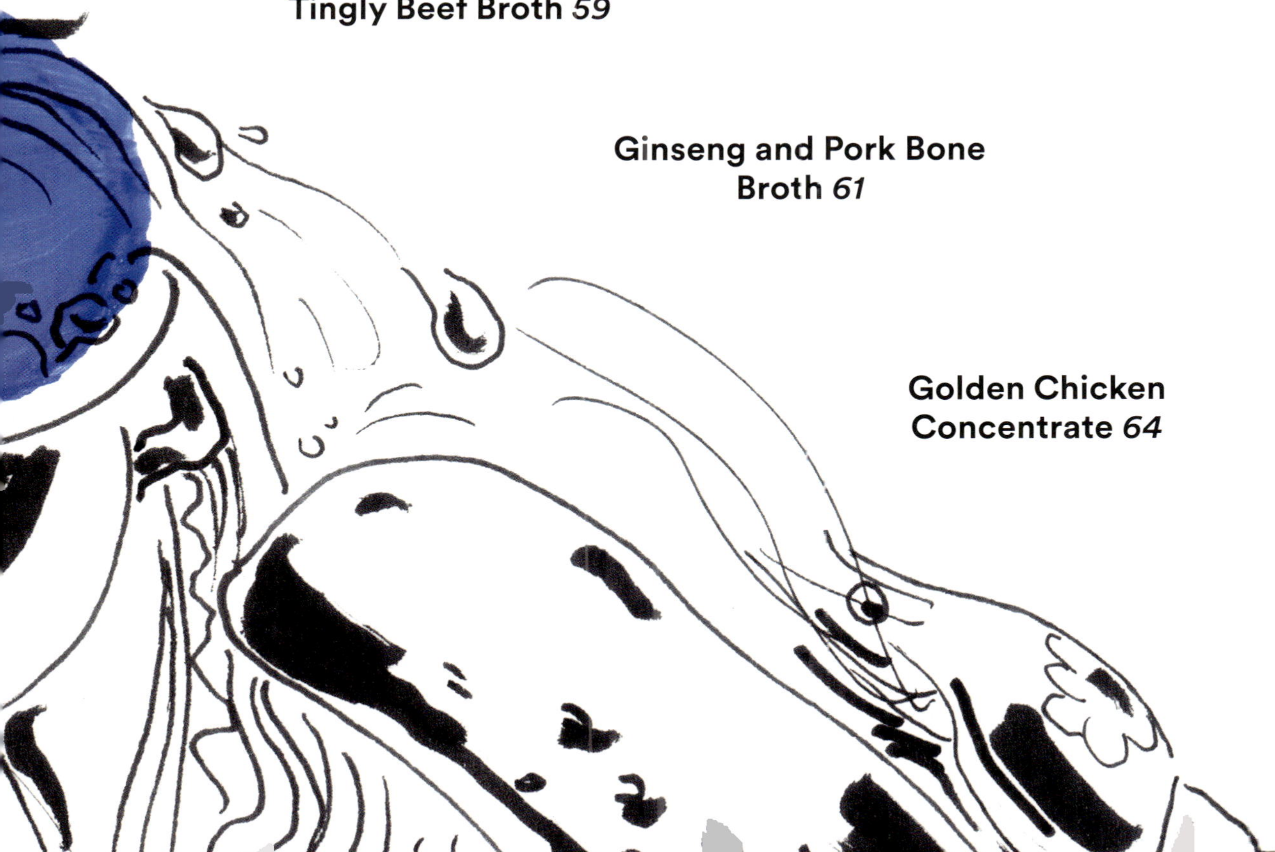

Broth is where this story really begins. This liquid—ranging from plain old water to an incendiary, fatty brew—embodies the range and versatility of hot pot itself. The broth sets the tone for what is to come and infiltrates its way into every morsel that enters your mouth. It can soothe and placate, refresh and revive. It can challenge your palate, setting it ablaze. Most important, it adds incredible depth of flavor and nuance to the numerous bites that bob and dance in it.

The best hot pot broths exude a certain point of view and symbolize the edifying harmony that is the backbone of hot pot philosophy. The broth is not a static object, either; throughout the course of the night, as you swish and dunk the ingredients on the table, the broth will ebb and flow, mutate and intensify. In this way, the broth becomes a communal project, and everyone at the table is a participant, an inadvertent chef, and a collaborator of this group soup.

At the table, the broth is a blank canvas, and you are the artist. Now is the time to choose small, decorative, floating objects that bob on the surface, creating playful patterns and adding their own essence. Fresh flowers, fruits, mushrooms, and herbs create a unique topography for your bites and add to the sensorial pleasures of the meal. Some hot pot restaurants employ hot pot vessels with two, three, four, or even nine chambers to hold different liquids. I highly recommend purchasing a dual-chambered hot pot, which allows you to curate two contrasting yet complementary broths (see page 19).

The recipes are scaled to produce enough broth for one round of hot pot. As the broth levels dip down throughout the course of the night, you'll refill the concentrated liquid with boiling-hot water, thus restoring balance to the pot. You can make the broth anytime and keep it frozen for those impromptu hot pot urges—you'll be so happy you did.

Hot Pot Bouillon

MAKES ¼ CUP (40 g) OF BOUILLON, ENOUGH FOR 2 QUARTS (1.9 L) OF BROTH

2 teaspoons mushroom powder

2 teaspoons nutritional yeast

1 teaspoon dark brown sugar

1 teaspoon Chinese Celery Salt (page 115)

1 teaspoon dried shrimp powder (from about 2 teaspoons whole dried shrimp)

1 teaspoon garlic powder (from about 2 teaspoons garlic chips)

1 teaspoon shallot powder (from about 2 teaspoons dried shallot pieces)

½ teaspoon ground ginger

½ teaspoon ground white pepper (from about 1 teaspoon whole white peppercorns)

Keep a jar of this instant hot pot seasoning in your pantry, at the ready to add surprising flavor and depth to any spur-of-the-moment hot pot cravings. If you're the type of person who hoards the seasoning packets from instant noodles, then you need this easy DIY bouillon in your repertoire.

First, you'll grind the dried shrimp, dried shallots, roasted garlic chips, and white peppercorns into a coarse powder. (A spice grinder or blender will do this nicely.) Then you'll whisk in all manner of dehydrated powders, like nutritional yeast, ginger, and mushroom. (If you can't find mushroom powder at the grocery store, look for freeze-dried or dried mushrooms, and pulverize those as finely as you can.) I like layering in each ingredient one at a time, like the sand art of my childhood, which makes the prettiest presents, too.

Combine the mushroom powder, nutritional yeast, brown sugar, Chinese Celery Salt, dried shrimp powder, garlic powder, shallot powder, ground ginger, and ground white pepper in a small airtight container. The mixture will keep for up to 3 months.

To activate in water, use 2 cups (480 ml) of water for every tablespoon of the bouillon powder. To prepare for hot pot, combine 2 quarts (1.9 L) of water and bouillon in a pot over high heat and bring to a boil. Reduce the heat, simmer for 5 minutes, then serve.

VARIATIONS

Try amending the basic bouillon formula with these unique additions.

- Oceanic and briny → 2 teaspoons dried kelp powder + 2 teaspoons dried bonito flakes
- Sneakily savory → substitute MSG for celery salt
- Mellow heat → 2 teaspoons ground gochugaru chile flakes
- Sweet and perfumed → 1 tablespoon Chinese five-spice powder
- 100% vegan → substitute 1 teaspoon dried white miso or dulse granules for dried shrimp

Mushroom Dashi

MAKES 2 QUARTS (1.9 L)

2½ quarts (2.4 L) filtered water

Two 8-inch (20 cm) pieces dried kombu

12 dried shiitake mushrooms (about 1 ounce/30 g)

1 bunch fresh scallions

1 cup (12 g) dried bonito flakes

HOT (POT) TIP Save the spent kombu for future meals—puree it with brown butter for a creamy spread (see page 86); finely chop it to fold into seaweed salads (see page 152); or toss it into a pot of steaming rice (see page 89).

FIND IT IN:
The Land and the Sea Feast (page 105)

If you're searching for a balanced, classical broth with a strong oceanic profile, look no further than dashi, a traditional Japanese soup broth made with dried kombu and bonito flakes (smoked and fermented skipjack tuna). This version gets an added earthiness from dried shiitakes and fresh scallions, two foundational hot pot ingredients. The flavor these simple pantry ingredients impart to water is so nourishing and deep—and a perfect complement for everything at your hot pot table.

Pour the water into a large pot. Add the dried kombu, dried shiitake mushrooms, and fresh scallions. Bring to a boil over high heat, then reduce the heat to low, cover, and simmer for 30 minutes.

Remove from the heat, add the dried bonito flakes, and stir gently. Let the flakes steep, like a tea, in the broth for 30 minutes. Then strain the liquid through a fine-mesh sieve, discarding the solids.

Use the broth immediately or store in an airtight container. It will keep for 1 week in the refrigerator or for up to 2 months in the freezer.

To prepare for hot pot, warm the broth, if needed, and then transfer to the hot pot topper. Garnish with a handful of dried mushrooms, if desired.

Tea Bag Broth

MAKES 4 TEA BAGS, ENOUGH FOR 4 QUARTS (3.8 L) OF BROTH

1 cup (50 g) dried shiitake mushrooms, sliced thinly

½ cup (20 g) green tea, like sencha or jasmine

⅓ cup (12 g) shredded dried kombu

¼ cup (35 g) whole white peppercorns

¼ cup (30 g) goji berries, plus more for garnish

¼ cup (35 g) dried onions

4 dried bay leaves

8 star anise pods

1 tablespoon kosher salt

EQUIPMENT

4 large spice sachets or tea bags at least 4 inches (10 cm) long

HOT (POT) TIP To go caffeine-free, replace the green tea with 1 cup (240 g) of an herbal tea, like lemongrass, chamomile, or roselle (Chinese hibiscus).

FIND IT IN:
The Endless Forest Feast (page 157)

Soup might be the greatest food of all time. It embraces frugality, resourcefulness, and harmony. It's nourishing, soothing, hydrating, and comforting. There's nothing more satisfying than a fridge sweep, pulling a little of this and that into a broth that is greater than the sum of its parts. And sometimes, a hot pot of green tea is the liquid to bring it all together. From Japanese ochazuke to Hakka Chinese leicha, or tea rice, there are many culinary dishes that use green tea to revive leftover steamed grains, alongside bits of vegetables, seaweed, fish, and nuts.

You can brew your own hot pot tea, too, which builds on the floral, earthy notes of green tea to create an aromatic, clean soup. It's as simple as filling empty tea bags with a medley of good green tea, dried aromatics, and spices. Submerge a bag into water just before commencing hot pot, and you'll have a rich, antioxidant-packed broth ready in minutes.

Combine the dried mushrooms, green tea, kombu, white peppercorns, goji berries, dried onions, bay leaves, star anise, and salt in a small bowl and stir to mix well. Divide the mixture evenly among the sachets. Seal them shut and store in an airtight container at room temperature for up to 2 months.

Each tea bag will yield 1 quart (950 ml) of broth. When you're ready for hot pot, bring 2 quarts (1.9 L) of water to a simmer. Add two tea bags and let steep, covered, for 10 minutes, then remove the tea bags and discard. Transfer the warm broth to the hot pot topper and garnish with an additional tablespoon of goji berries, if desired.

Charred Tomato and Lemongrass Broth

MAKES 2 QUARTS (1.9 L)

1 white onion, halved

One 14.5-ounce (410 g) can fire-roasted tomatoes

2 quarts (1.9 L) filtered water

One 2-inch (5 cm) piece fresh ginger, peeled and sliced into ¼-inch-thick (0.6 cm) rounds

Four 6-inch (15 cm) lemongrass stalks, halved lengthwise

2 celery stalks

2 tablespoons olive oil

2 tablespoons tomato paste

6 Thai chiles or 1 teaspoon ground gochugaru chile flakes, plus more for garnish (see Tip)

2 teaspoons kosher salt

Juice of 1 lime

1 beefsteak or heirloom tomato, for garnish

HOT (POT) TIP Thai chile, a small, spicy pepper that turns from green to red as it ripens, can be found in many Asian grocery stores. Keep a surplus in the refrigerator for perking up broth, slicing thinly into simple dipping sauces (see page 116), or jazzing up pickle brines (see page 138).

Craving hot pot on a long, steamy day? This broth, full of bright, jumpy acidic notes and a low, sweet, smoky char, is perfect for sipping outdoors under the bright sun. Lemongrass adds a citrusy tang; at Asian grocery stores, you can usually find the stalks both fresh and frozen, or processed into powders, teas, and paste (you'll need about 1 tablespoon of paste or 2 tablespoons of dried lemongrass for every 2 quarts/1.9 L of water). Instead of charring fresh tomatoes yourself, look for fire-roasted canned varieties—they're just as delicious.

Heat a large pot over medium heat for 3 to 4 minutes. Place the onion halves, cut side down, in the pot and let sizzle, untouched, until they are blackened, 5 minutes.

While the onion halves are charring, puree the canned tomatoes with an immersion or tabletop blender until smooth.

Add the tomato puree and water to the pot, along with the sliced ginger, lemongrass, celery, olive oil, tomato paste, Thai chiles, and salt. Bring to a boil over high heat, then reduce the heat to very low, cover, and let barely simmer, until slightly reduced and the onion and celery are translucent and supersoft, 2 to 3 hours.

Remove the pot from the heat and strain the broth through a fine-mesh sieve, discarding the solids. Stir in the lime juice.

Use the broth immediately or store in an airtight container. It will keep for 1 week in the refrigerator or for up to 2 months in the freezer.

FIND IT IN:
The Endless Forest Feast
(page 157)

→

To prepare for hot pot, warm the broth, if needed, and then transfer to the hot pot topper. Slice the tomato into rounds about ¼ inch (0.6 cm) thick. Drop the slices into the broth, like lily pads, and add a few fresh Thai chiles.

VARIATIONS

- If you aren't able to find canned fire-roasted tomatoes, roast fresh ones yourself: Slice 6 ripe tomatoes in half lengthwise and broil until their edges are blackened and blistered, 3 to 4 minutes.
- For extra-rich creaminess, whisk one 8-ounce (226 g) can of full-fat, unsweetened coconut milk into the warm broth, along with the lime juice, then transfer to your hot pot topper.
- Lacto-fermented condiments are a powerful "secret" ingredient for many Asian soups, adding tangy complexity and depth. For an extra punchy, sour note, add ¼ cup of whey, chopped sauerkraut or kimchi, a teaspoon of hot sauce, or a tablespoon of dark miso paste to the broth.

Royal Chrysanthemum Broth

MAKES 2 QUARTS (1.9 L)

1 bunch fresh scallions

2 garlic heads

1 carrot

One 1-inch (2.5 cm) piece ginger

3 quarts (2.8 L) filtered water

30 dried shiitake mushrooms (about 3½ ounces/100 g)

2 tablespoons goji berries

½ bunch fresh cilantro, stems only

¼ cup (60 ml) Shaoxing wine

2 teaspoons kosher salt

2 teaspoons soy sauce

1 teaspoon whole black peppercorns

¼ cup (15 g) dried chrysanthemum tea

HOT (POT) TIP Save the softened shiitake mushrooms to serve at hot pot, or use them for dumpling fillings (see page 91) or sliced thinly and folded into marinated mushroom salads (see page 155).

FIND IT IN:
This Heat Feast (page 187)

Chrysanthemums are one of the most beloved flowers in Chinese history, their densely patterned blooms long regarded as a symbol of longevity, wealth, and vitality. Coveted for both their medicinal properties and singular beauty, chrysanthemums were known to be scattered over the surface of palatial hot pots, as they were thought to have life-extending, immune-boosting powers.

These days, chrysanthemum flowers are most commonly consumed as a dried tea and can be easily found at Asian grocery stores or tea parlors while their (also edible and delicious in their own right) leafy greens are popular in stir-fries and soups. Here, when paired with dried shiitake mushrooms, a cornerstone of Chinese cuisine, a complex, aromatic, and nourishing broth emerges. Sweetness and acidity are added to counterweight the earthiness of the shiitakes and the cooling, unfurling bitterness of the tea, which is added right before beginning hot pot.

Chop the green tops off the scallions and (if you plan to use the broth in the next few days) set them aside for garnishing. Slice the white bottoms in half lengthwise. Chop the garlic heads, carrot, and ginger in half as well, which will help release their flavor into the broth.

Combine the water, scallion whites, garlic, carrot, ginger, dried shiitake mushrooms, goji berries, cilantro stems, Shaoxing wine, salt, soy sauce, and black peppercorns in a large pot. Bring the mixture to a boil over high heat, then reduce the heat to very low and simmer gently until the broth has reduced to about 2 quarts (1.9 L) and the carrot is soft, about 1 hour.

Remove the pot from the heat and let the broth cool completely, several hours or overnight, before straining, pressing out as much of the liquid from the softened vegetables as you can (see Tip). →

Opposites Attract (*from left*): *The Tingly Beef Broth and Royal Chrysanthemum Broth, with their contrasting flavor profiles, are a delicious pairing for a two-chambered hot pot.*

Use the broth immediately or store in an airtight container. It will keep for 1 week in the refrigerator or for up to 2 months in the freezer.

To prepare for hot pot, warm the broth and then transfer to the hot pot topper. Chop the reserved scallion greens into 2-inch-long (5 cm) batons and add to the broth, along with the dried chrysanthemum tea.

Tingly Beef Broth

MAKES 3 QUARTS (2.8 L)

½ cup (120 ml) vegetable oil

3 pounds (1.4 kg) beef neck bones, cut into 2- to 3-inch (5 to 7.5 cm) pieces

1 small yellow onion, halved

1 shallot, halved

1 apple, halved

2 medium carrots

1 garlic head, halved crosswise

One 3-inch (7.5 cm) piece ginger, roughly chopped

2 cups (60 g) dried Sichuan chiles, plus 1 cup (30 g) for garnish

4 tablespoons (60 g) spicy Sichuan chile bean paste

¼ cup Sichuan peppercorns

2 tablespoons fermented black beans

2 tablespoons ground gochugaru chile flakes

4 dried bay leaves

4 star anise pods

2 cinnamon sticks

1 teaspoon whole cloves

1 teaspoon cumin seeds

1 teaspoon fennel seeds

½ cup (120 ml) Shaoxing wine

4 quarts (3.8 L) filtered water

Facing Heaven chile peppers, or chao tian jiao—so-called for the way they grow, with their cone-shaped tips pointed upward to the sky—are a culinary icon of the province of Sichuan, where they are grown in the capital city of Chengdu. Though these chiles may look fierce when bobbing on the surface of a hot pot broth, their bark is stronger than their bite. Because they're only about medium hot, they're used in everything from soup bases to stir-fries to long braises, often in concert with other, more intense ingredients—including that other icon of Sichuan cuisine, Sichuan peppercorns, which are actually the berries from an ash tree. These little flavor bombs have a distinct mouth-numbing quality, or mala; there's nothing else quite like it.

A hot pot broth made with all these maximal flavors often uses beef or pork bones to add richness and body, and even additional tallow, or beef fat, to further enhance the shimmering broth. This version uses beef neck bones, which release nourishing amounts of collagen into the water as they cook, though you can also use larger marrow bones or meatier bones like short rib or oxtails.

The most common type of hot pot "base," or huoguo diliao, that you can find in a grocery store is usually the Sichuan mala style. Vacuum-sealed and scored into neon-red bricks, these shelf-stable packs feature a bounty of spices and chiles suspended in solid fat. While these are affordable and easily sourced, you'll love making the broth yourself—and the rolling clouds of fragrant steam it releases as it simmers.

Pour the vegetable oil into a large stockpot set over medium heat (it should be able to comfortably hold at least 6 quarts/5.7 L). Once the oil is shimmering, add the beef bones and sear, untouched, for 4 to 5 minutes on each side, rotating with tongs, until deeply golden brown on all sides.

→

HOT (POT) TIP

Spicy Sichuan chile bean paste combines fruity chile peppers with fermented soybeans and other seasonings to make a fragrant, umami-rich condiment that enlivens everything from soup to noodles to dumplings. It's a must for your DIY sauce bar, too (see page 128).

Remove the bones from the pot and transfer to a baking sheet to make room for the next batch of ingredients. Add the onion, shallot, apple, carrots, garlic, and ginger to the hot oil. Fry until charred and deeply browned in places, 10 minutes. Remove with tongs or a slotted spoon and add to the baking sheet.

Next, add the Sichuan chiles, Sichuan chile bean paste, Sichuan peppercorns, fermented black beans, gochugaru, bay leaves, star anise, cinnamon sticks, cloves, cumin seeds, and fennel seeds to the pot. Cook, stirring continuously, for 1 to 2 minutes.

Add the Shaoxing wine to deglaze the pot, and top with the water. Bring to a boil over high heat, then immediately reduce to a very low simmer. Return the reserved bones and aromatics to the pot. Maintain a low simmer—just a few bubbles popping along the surface—until the liquid has reduced by one-third and the vegetables are soft and pale, 5 to 6 hours.

Remove the broth from the heat and let cool completely. Strain through a fine-mesh sieve, discarding the solids.

Use the broth immediately or store in an airtight container. It will keep for 4 days in the refrigerator or for up to 2 months in the freezer.

To prepare for hot pot, warm the broth, if needed, and transfer to the hot pot topper. Top the broth with another 1 cup (30 g) of dried Sichuan chiles, as a garnish.

Ginseng and Pork Bone Broth

MAKES 3 QUARTS (2.8 L)

1 pound (450 g) pork ribs, neck bones, or similar

10 ounces (280 g) chicken wing tips or feet

6 Chinese celery stalks

6 dried jujubes (see Resources, page 214)

1 American ginseng root (about 50 g; see Tip)

1 large or 2 small carrots, halved

1 bunch fresh scallions

4 quarts filtered water (3.8 L)

1 tablespoon kosher salt

FIND IT IN:
The Land and the Sea Feast (page 105)

Chinese cuisine places great importance on harmony—even with recipes as quotidian as stock. Just one sip reveals how fresh aromatics brighten rich elements, or how bitter or sour notes are countered with sweet or savory ingredients. This philosophy of balance is invaluable when handling tricky ingredients like ginseng root, which has a bitter, bracing flavor. But when ginseng is paired with warming ingredients, like jujubes, a kind of Chinese date, and rich pork bones, something delicious and nourishing emerges.

Clear, non-spicy hot pot broths (or qingtang guodi) are typically made with a mix of chicken, pork, or beef bones, simmered over very low heat alongside aromatics and herbal elements. The slow-cooking method ensures a crystalline appearance and maximum flavor.

Place the pork and chicken bones in a stockpot and add enough water to cover them. Bring to a boil over high heat and let boil for 5 minutes to draw out any impurities. Transfer the bones to a bowl, discard the water, and rinse out the pot.

Place the bones back in the pot and add the celery, dried jujubes, ginseng, carrot, and the scallions. Cover with the water and bring to a boil over high heat. As soon as the liquid reaches a boil, reduce the heat to low, until a steady sprinkling of bubbles forms along the surface. Simmer for 3 to 4 hours, or for up to 6 hours, until the broth is golden and the carrot and celery look limp and translucent.

Remove the pot from the heat and stir in the salt.

Let the broth cool completely, then cover and transfer to the refrigerator to chill overnight. The next day, gently warm the pot over very low heat to loosen the gelatin

HOT (POT) TIP

Ginseng is a precious plant in China, where it has been revered as a cornerstone of traditional Chinese medicine for thousands of years. The name "ginseng" doesn't denote a specific plant but rather is an umbrella term for many different varieties, from American ginseng (prized for its cooling and sedative medicinal effects, or yin) to Asian ginseng (fiery and strong, or yang). Dried ginseng root (the kind you'd use for tea), sold either as slices or granulated, is easy to find in grocery stores, but check the produce section of Asian supermarkets for fresh American-grown ginseng. While it's expensive, a little bit goes a long way (and you can store any extra in the freezer for safekeeping). If you can't find any, feel free to substitute with dried ginseng root, but you'll need about twice as much.

wobble and then strain the broth through a fine-mesh sieve, reserving the ginseng root and jujubes; you should have about 3 quarts (2.8 L) of broth.

Use the broth immediately or store in an airtight container. It will keep for 4 days in the refrigerator or for up to 2 months in the freezer.

To prepare for hot pot, warm the broth, if needed, and then transfer to the hot pot topper, adding the ginseng root and jujubes back to the soup.

Golden Chicken Concentrate

MAKES 2½ QUARTS (2.4 L)

6 Chinese celery stalks, plus leaves

1 large carrot

One 3-inch (7.5 cm) piece ginger

1 bunch fresh scallions

2 pounds (910 g) chicken feet

1 garlic head, halved crosswise

3 dried bay leaves

8 star anise pods

2 teaspoons whole white peppercorns

2 teaspoons kosher salt

4 quarts (3.8 L) filtered water, plus 2 cups (480 ml) for serving

For a truly superior hot pot soup, look no further than this golden-hued elixir, which has an unmatched, soulful richness. Thanks to collagen-rich chicken feet, this silky broth uniquely coats your lips and tongue, leaving a glistening ring of moisture and fat.

Roughly chop the celery, carrot, ginger, and scallions into large chunks and transfer to a large stockpot (it should be able to comfortably hold at least 6 quarts/5.7 L).

Add the chicken feet, garlic, bay leaves, star anise, white peppercorns, and salt and cover with 4 quarts (3.8 L) of water. Bring to a boil over high heat. As soon as the water reaches a boil, reduce the heat to a very low simmer—you want just a few bubbles popping along the surface.

Gently simmer until the volume has reduced by nearly half, and the celery and carrots are supersoft, 4 hours. Occasionally run a spoon across the surface of the broth to remove scum.

Let the broth cool completely, then cover and transfer to the refrigerator to chill overnight. The next day, gently warm the pot over very low heat, then strain the broth through a fine-mesh sieve, discarding the solids.

Use the broth immediately or store in an airtight container. It will keep for 4 days in the refrigerator or for up to 2 months in the freezer.

To prepare for hot pot, warm the broth, if needed, and then transfer to the hot pot topper. Dilute with an additional 2 cups (480 ml) of water.

VARIATIONS

This broth is like the little black dress of soup—dress it up or down, it goes with absolutely everything.

- Chinese five-spice powder → 1 tablespoon fennel seeds + 1 tablespoon whole cloves + 4 Chinese cinnamon sticks
- Bright acidity → ¼ cup (65 g) tomato paste + ¼ cup (60 ml) Shaoxing wine
- Spicy → 1 cup (30 g) dried Sichuan chiles + 2 tablespoons ground gochugaru chile flakes

HOT POT FEAST NO. 1

The Northern Classic

In Beijing, where my mother grew up, hot pot is an essential ritual for enduring the long, bitterly cold winter months. The meal incorporates culinary traditions from both northeastern China and Mongolia, with a focus on affordable ingredients like tofu and napa cabbage.

When my mom immigrated to the United States in the early 1980s, she brought hot pot with her. My parents' signature hot pot feasts start with a base of filtered water, rather than a strongly seasoned, fatty broth. The quality of purchased ingredients, like leafy greens and tender meat, is the focus here. The endless, communal dipping and swishing of the savory morsels enriches the water, resulting in a transportive broth.

Though some hot pot aficionados insist on cooking ingredients in a specific order, I prefer to kick-start the broth by adding aromatic vegetables—like chunks of cabbage, coins of carrot, dried shiitake mushrooms, and scallion stalks—right away. Though you're free to supplement the menu or make substitutions with your favorite ingredients and recipes, don't lose sight of this special, restorative meal: a clear, light broth; lean, strong-tasting meats; an array of simple, hearty vegetables; and the iconic white sesame dipping sauce.

GET READY

The day before (or up to 2 weeks in advance), shape and freeze the Not-Just-Scallion Pancakes (page 83) and the Shrimp and Pea Shoot Dumplings (page 99). The Toasted Cumin and White Sesame Sauce (page 122) greatly improves overnight, so mix that, too.

The day of the party, prep all the hot pot ingredients, and plate the Cucumber and Peanut Pyramids (page 151) shortly before guests arrive.

THE TABLESIDE STRATEGY

Don't forget the finale (my family's favorite moment of the night): the concluding bowl of communal broth. What starts as water will be a totally unique and nourishing soup, thickened by the residual pools of white sesame sauce.

HOT (POT) TIP

It's not hot pot unless there's a small dish of salted peanuts nearby. Look for red-skinned Chinese varieties online and in stores; they typically come in small containers or vacuum-sealed pouches and are crunchy, not greasy, and highly addictive. Our family also favors the Huang Fei Hong brand of spicy peanuts, which comes laced with MSG, shards of red chili pepper, and mouth-numbing Sichuan peppercorn. Buy multiple bags—you'll be so glad you did.

Pickled and Fermented Hot Pot Surprises

When it comes to Beijing-style hot pot, store-bought Chinese condiments are essential tools for building flavor. Pickled mustard greens, usually spiked with garlic, chiles, or peppercorns, add an unctuous, mustardy funk to poached meats and noodles. Look for vacuum-sealed pouches in the produce section or shelf-stable glass jars by the condiments.

Fermented tofu is another quintessential Chinese staple—and a personal favorite. It smooths the edges of savory ingredients, especially when whisked into dipping sauces, where it all but disappears, leaving a pleasantly fruity sweetness behind (it always makes me think of pineapple gummy bears).

Salted leek flowers, sometimes labeled as "chive paste," can be spooned over boiled mutton or lamb, draping each bite with a palate-balancing brightness *(see Resources, page 214)**.*

HARBIN

THE MENU

EQUIPMENT LIST (see page 18)

KNIFE CUTS AND COOKING INSTRUCTIONS (see page 27)

RUN OF SHOW (see page 40)

THE "BROTH"

4 quarts (3.8 L) filtered water, plus more to top off

THE SAUCE

Toasted Cumin and White Sesame Sauce (page 122)

THE STARCHES

Not-Just-Scallion Pancakes (page 83)

Shrimp and Pea Shoot Dumplings (page 99)

THE SALAD

Cucumber and Peanut Pyramids (page 151)

THE DRINK

Baijiu Shooters (page 208)

THE DESSERT

Double Mango Jelly (page 167)

THE SPREAD

Kabocha and tofu skin skewers (page 39)

8 ounces (230 g) sliced lamb shoulder

8 ounces (230 g) sliced lamb leg

8 ounces (230 g) sliced beef, like top sirloin or rib eye

4 ounces (115 g) beef tripe, sliced

4 ounces (115 g) firm tofu, cubed

1 head napa cabbage, chopped (about 1⅓ pounds/600 g)

4 ounces (115 g) snow pea shoots or similar (choose from The Hot Pot Ingredient Guide, page 28)

1 bunch fresh scallions, diced

1 bunch fresh cilantro, chopped

2 bundles bean thread noodles

The Lucky 8 Hot Pot Personalities

AT A RAMBUNCTIOUS hot pot table, distinct personality types emerge—you know it when you see it. Which one are you?

THE DIRECTOR

A natural leader, you take charge with the offerings, telling everyone which meat and sauce combo is the best, opening multiple bottles of wine, and introducing all the guests to each other. You love to sit next to a Newbie and show them the way.

THE TOASTER

You love to grandstand. You give long, winding speeches throughout the night, always ending with a shot of baijiu and a rousing cheer of *gan bei*!

THE MOTHER

You can't help it—you love to take care of others. Instead of feeding yourself, you dump bites of food into the pot and then deposit them in someone else's bowl.

THE AMNESIAC

Though well intentioned, your absent-minded nature leads you to forget bites of food you dropped into the broth. If they're not fished out by someone else, they turn sad and soggy by the night's end. Be sure to sit next to a Mother!

THE GIFTER

You never show up to a hot pot party without a crate of fancy fruit, box of Ferrero Rocher, or fluffy layer cake from your favorite Chinese bakery.

THE NEWBIE

This is your first time at the hot pot table. Many consider you the guest of honor! You follow everyone else's lead—asking for tips on making the perfect dipping sauce, setting a stopwatch to prevent overcooking bites, and secretly looking up the names of unfamiliar ingredients.

THE PARTIER

You're in charge of the playlist, the lighting, and the vibe. You're dressed impeccably, and have been known to introduce drinking games at the table, raffle off small gifts throughout the night, and draw dirty words into the fogged-up windows.

THE GERMAPHOBE

You remind everyone that the large chopsticks are for handling bites, not for personal use. You like to "disinfect" your personal chopsticks in the boiling broth, and you're never without hand sanitizer or wet wipes.

BREADS, DUMPLINGS & RICE

Delicious, Sating Starches

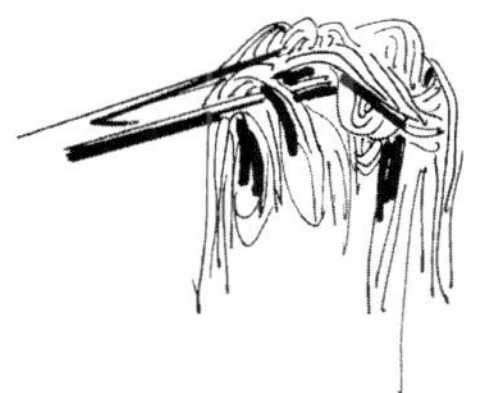

When I was a kid I was obsessed with hot pot, but not because I loved soup, or even the chaos of cooking my own food. It was for the endless baskets of crisp, golden scallion pancakes, or cong you bing, that were passed around the table. I couldn't resist those warm, palm-sized breads, especially after dragging one through a puddle of black vinegar or white sesame sauce.

Chewy, Chinese-style flatbreads, served alongside hot pot, are like the garlic bread to your spaghetti or the tortilla chips to your chili. These are dough-based, hand-stretched creations designed to soak up sauce, bathe in broth, and add heft to your meal.

A pocket-sized bread acts as a handheld utensil, cradling bites or wiping plates clean. The Kombu and Brown Butter Texas Toast (page 86) absorbs flavorful broth, its buttery surface a rich complement to slices of meat or bean curd. In a hot oven, the Black and White Shaobing (page 79) puffs up like a pita; you'll open it up lengthwise, filling the hollow crevice with boiled noodles, herbs, and tofu—a bonus soup-and-sandwich combination.

Dumplings, the ultimate comfort food, belong with hot pot, too. Though there are a million alluring options in the supermarket freezer aisles, making them yourself is a righteous act of care and craft. Shaping your own dumplings is a creative opportunity for you to make a perfectly balanced bite—is there anything better than a frilly parcel stuffed with a vibrant blend of herbs and vegetables?—while meditating on the repetitive movements of stuffing, pleating, and sealing. During hot pot, the dumplings swell and soak up the flavorful soup, and whether you choose an entirely vegan filling (see page 91) or one rich with seafood (see page 96), it's immensely satisfying.

Though modern-day Chinese hot pot is not typically associated with the consumption of steamed white rice, it actually has origins as a pragmatic working-class meal meant to be eaten with rice. Steamed rice is the perfect starch to absorb the nuanced flavors of hot pot soup, and it is great to feed a crowd. Adding nutty, tender mung beans to jasmine rice results in a hearty, nutritious pilaf (see page 89) that pairs exceptionally well with hot pot.

Black and White Shaobing

MAKES SIX 5-INCH (13 CM) FLATBREADS

1 cup (240 ml) filtered water

2 cups (240 g) bread flour

1 tablespoon sugar

1 teaspoon kosher salt

½ teaspoon instant dry yeast

1 tablespoon vegetable oil

1 recipe Black Sesame Sauce (recipe follows), at room temperature

⅓ cup (45 g) white sesame seeds

⅓ cup (45 g) black sesame seeds

1 egg white, lightly beaten

Flaky sea salt, to finish

FIND IT IN:
This Heat Feast (page 187)

PAIR IT WITH:
Napa cabbage, Toasted Cumin and White Sesame Sauce (page 122)

Freshly baked shaobing—a hand-stretched, layered flatbread, usually coated with sesame seeds, and stuffed with everything from red bean paste to braised pork—is a hallmark of northern Chinese cuisine and a quintessential hot pot accompaniment. Most breads in this style are baked in a very hot oven, where the heat creates steam in the oil-enriched dough, resulting in a puffed, chewy pastry with distinct layers. On the hot pot table, its presence is somewhat strategic: Its flaky, airy structure is the perfect purse to cradle morsels that emerge from the broth.

Pour the water into a small pot or teakettle and heat until boiling.

Combine the flour, sugar, salt, and yeast in a medium bowl. Slowly stream in the hot water, stirring until a loose dough forms.

Add the vegetable oil and begin to knead by hand; the dough will be very loose, wet, and stretchy. Continue to knead the dough, pulling it up into the air and slapping it down on the counter, for 5 minutes.

Gently shape the dough into a round and transfer to a small bowl. Drape with plastic wrap and let rest in the refrigerator for at least 30 minutes, or for up to 4 hours.

On a clean, lightly oiled countertop, stretch the dough out to a rectangle about 16 inches (40 cm) wide and 20 inches (50 cm) long. Start stretching it out with a rolling pin; you can also very carefully stretch the dough with oiled fingertips, gently tugging from underneath and stretching it outward. (Don't worry at all if the dough tears a little.) The dough should look thin and sheer.

→

HOT (POT) TIP

No time to knead? This dough can be mixed in a food processor, too. Combine the flour, sugar, salt, and yeast in the bowl of a food processor. With the food processor running, stream in the boiling water and vegetable oil, and continue to mix until the dough has formed into a sticky ball, about 10 seconds. Scrape the dough out of the processor onto the counter. Sprinkle with more oil and gently shape the dough into a ball. Cover with a towel or plastic wrap and let rest for 30 minutes, while the dough cools. Proceed with the rest of the recipe as written.

Pinch the black sesame sauce all over the surface of the dough, using your fingertips to smear it in. Starting from the bottom, and working your way from left to right, roll the dough up tightly, like a jelly roll; you should end up with a log about 24 inches (60 cm) long.

Using a bench scraper or small serrated knife, divide the dough into six pieces. (The easiest way to do this is to slice the log in half and then divide each half into three pieces.)

To shape each piece, tuck the cut ends underneath, pinching them closed. Flatten the top with the heel of your hand, then roll each piece into a rectangle 5 inches (12.5 cm) long and 3 inches (7.5 cm) wide.

At this point, you can partially freeze the shaobing on a baking sheet lined with parchment paper, then stack them in an airtight container in the freezer for up to 3 weeks.

If you're baking them right away, preheat the oven to 400°F (205°C). Line a baking sheet with parchment paper.

Pour the black and white sesame seeds onto a plate. Brush the shaobing with egg white, then press the moistened surface onto the sesame seeds, so they firmly stick (about 2 tablespoons of sesame seeds per bread). Add a pinch of flaky sea salt to the surface. Transfer to the lined baking sheet, allowing about 3 inches (7.5 cm) of space for each shaobing. Repeat with the remaining dough pieces.

Bake until the edges are lightly browned, 16 to 18 minutes. Eat immediately, while piping hot.

Black Sesame Sauce

MAKES A SCANT ½ CUP (110 g)

½ cup (60 g) bread flour

2 tablespoons black sesame paste

2 tablespoons sesame oil

1 tablespoon vegetable oil

½ teaspoon kosher salt

Combine the flour, black sesame paste, sesame oil, vegetable oil, and salt in a small skillet over medium-low heat. Work the mixture with a spatula until evenly combined and cook, stirring occassionally, 3 to 4 minutes. Scrape the mixture into a small bowl and let cool completely. Transfer to an airtight container and store in the refrigerator for up to 2 weeks.

Black and White and Delicious All Over

A stretchy, resilient dough forms the base of this flaky bread. The dough is stretched into a translucent sheet then painted with a nutty sauce. The flaky layers are formed from its coiled, jelly roll shaping, which can all be done by hand—no special gear required.

Not-Just-Scallion Pancakes

MAKES FOUR 8-INCH (20 CM) PANCAKES

1 cup (240 ml) filtered water

1 cup (about 30 g) packed fresh herbs (like scallions, basil, parsley, mint, tarragon, cilantro, sorrel, or dill)

2 cups (240 g) all-purpose flour

1 teaspoon kosher salt

About ¼ cup (60 ml) vegetable oil, for cooking and shaping

¼ cup (60 ml) sesame oil

Flaky sea salt, to finish

Black and Brown Vinegar, for dipping (page 116)

FIND IT IN:
The Northern Classic Feast (page 67)

PAIR IT WITH:
Black and Brown Vinegar (page 116)

The archetypal green onion pancake, or cong you bing—an unleavened flatbread swirled with chopped alliums—is a symphony of textural pleasure. There are the browned edges that shatter into fragments; the spiraled surface, pocked with leopard spots; the chewy, almost doughy center, rich with oil.

The shaping method is a revelation if you're used to American-style lamination. To make cong you bing, hot water "seizes" the proteins in the flour, resulting in a smooth, resilient, relaxed dough that is a breeze to roll and twist into shapes and strong enough to hold all manner of fillings.

Here, instead of just sticking to the classical green onion seasoning, you'll use up *all* of those wilting herbs in your refrigerator, each one contributing its own unique essence.

Pour the water into a small pot and heat until boiling.

Meanwhile, finely chop the fresh herbs into confetti; measured tightly in a cup, the herbs should collapse to yield about ⅓ cup.

Combine the flour and salt in a medium bowl. Slowly stream in the hot water, stirring with chopsticks until a loose dough forms. Once the dough is cool enough to handle, bring this shaggy mixture together by hand, kneading for a minute or two.

Shape the dough into a rough ball; it will be sticky. Cover and let rest in the refrigerator to chill for at least 30 minutes and up to 8 hours.

Using a big knife or bench scraper, divide the dough into quarters, each weighing about 4½ ounces (125 g). Form a hand into a claw, like you're holding an invisible baseball, then roll the dough pieces into smooth balls.

→

HOT (POT) TIP

Don't want to transfer savory smells like sesame oil or chopped alliums to your rolling pin? Roll each pancake between two squares of parchment about 12 inches (30 cm) wide.

Lightly grease a rolling pin and your work surface with vegetable oil. Roll a piece of dough into a circle about 10 inches (25 cm) wide; the dough will be very thin and sheer. Brush the dough circle with a thin coating of sesame oil (about 1 teaspoon), and top with a heaping tablespoon of the chopped herbs.

Starting with the bottom of the circle, roll up the dough, like a scroll or a jelly roll. Twist the scroll into a tight spiral, like a snail's shell, as it lies flat on your work surface.

Repeat with the remaining dough. Drape a dish cloth over all the dough spirals and let rest for 30 minutes.

Line a large baking sheet with parchment paper. Roll each dough spiral into a circle about 8 inches (20 cm) wide, adding a little vegetable oil to the rolling pin if the dough feels overly sticky or tears. Stack the circles on the lined baking sheet as you go, separating each one with a small square of parchment. The pancakes shouldn't feel overly sticky or wet, but it's okay if the herbs slightly tear the dough while you're rolling it out. (Note: Don't roll the pancakes too thinly, which would compress their flaky layers and result in more of a cracker.)

At this point, you can partially freeze the pancakes on a baking sheet lined with parchment paper, then stack them in an airtight container in the freezer for up to 3 weeks.

When you're ready to cook the pancakes, heat 1 tablespoon of vegetable oil in a large skillet over medium heat. Set a baking sheet lined with a dry towel nearby as a place for the pancakes to land and drain once removed from the oil.

Fry the pancakes one at a time, 4 to 5 minutes for each pancake, flipping halfway through and replenishing the oil after each round. Transfer to the towel-lined baking sheet and sprinkle with flaky sea salt.

Using a sharp cleaver or chef's knife, cut each pancake in half, then cut each half into 1-inch (2.5 cm) wide strips. Serve immediately with Black and Brown Vinegar on the side, for dipping.

Twist and Shout: Creating Flaky Layers with a Snail-Like Technique

This method stretches a lean dough into paper-thin rounds, which get painted with fat and dressed with herbs. Each flatbread is rolled up like a scroll, coiled around like a snail, and pressed into a wide pancake; every twist and tug of the dough ensures a flaky, pull-apart texture once it's fried in a shallow pool of oil.

Kombu and Brown Butter Texas Toast

MAKES 8 SERVINGS AND ½ CUP (130 g) BUTTER

8 tablespoons (1 stick/110 g) unsalted butter

2 tablespoons (5 g) dried kombu (from about one 3-inch/7.5 cm sheet, broken up or shredded)

½ cup (120 ml) filtered water

1 tablespoon white miso paste

1 teaspoon soy sauce

8 thick slices Asian milk bread

Asian milk bread, or shokupan—a feathery, pillowy loaf enriched with milk, eggs, or butter—is engineered to become the thick hot pot toast of your dreams. A grocery-bought loaf of milk bread, already portioned into fat, squishy, 1-inch-thick (2.5 cm) slices, is the perfect swap for that great buttery, garlicky barbecue accompaniment known as Texas toast. (This is not the time to use a crusty artisan sourdough.)

Velvety slices of bread are spread with a simple compound butter, inspired by the popular Japanese preserve tsukudani, a salty, inky spread of softened seaweed. Here the sweet nuttiness of brown butter is married with the dusky, fermented notes of soy sauce, miso paste, and boiled kombu. Slathered thickly onto milk bread, then toasted until deeply golden and crisp, it's the perfect snack on its own, but, as you can imagine, even better with hot pot.

Melt the butter in a small skillet over medium heat. After 2 to 3 minutes, the butter will heavily foam and bubble. As the milk solids settle to the bottom of the pan, the foam will burn off. Once the milk solids are a golden brown, about 2 additional minutes, and the air smells nutty and sweet, remove the pan from the heat. Carefully pour the butter into a small bowl, scraping all of the browned milk solids from the bottom of the pan and adding those, too. Transfer to the fridge to chill until opaque, yet yielding to the touch, about 20 minutes.

Meanwhile, combine the dried kombu with the water in a small pot and simmer until softened, 3 to 4 minutes. Drain out the water (or save for the Mushroom Dashi, page 50), reserving 1 tablespoon.

Puree the softened kombu and the reserved tablespoon of kombu water in the bowl of a food processor until chunky and paste-like (or mash it up with a mortar and pestle).

FIND IT IN:
The Land and the Sea Feast (page 105)

PAIR IT WITH:
Charred and Candied Orange Sauce (page 121), shrimp, kabocha squash, chrysanthemum greens

HOT (POT) TIP

Spread the milk bread with the kombu butter, then arrange the slices on a sheet pan and freeze for 10 minutes. Stack up the slices, wrap tightly, and freeze for up to 3 weeks. When you're ready for toast, add on an additional minute under the broiler or in your sauté pan, but otherwise proceed exactly as written.

Add the browned butter, white miso paste, and soy sauce and puree until smooth and fluffy, 1 to 2 minutes.

Use immediately, or transfer to an airtight container and store in the refrigerator for up to 2 weeks or the freezer for up to 1 month.

To make the Texas toast, preheat a toaster oven or broiler. Spread the room-temperature kombu butter on each side of the milk bread slices, 1 teaspoon per side. Toast until golden brown and crisp, about 1 minute on each side, directly under the broiler. (Alternatively, griddle the bread in a pan over medium-high heat, about 1½ minutes on each side.)

Use a serrated knife to slice the toast into three batons; serve immediately.

OFF
AUTO EJECTION

Mung Bean and Rice Pilaf

MAKES 4 CUPS (ABOUT 800 g)

⅓ cup (70 g) dried whole mung beans (see Tips)

2 cups plus 2 tablespoons (510 ml) filtered water

1 cup (200 g) jasmine rice

½ teaspoon kosher salt

2 teaspoons rice vinegar

1 teaspoon toasted sesame oil

1 teaspoon soy sauce

A handful of fresh herbs (optional)

1 tangerine (optional)

A handful of dried goji berries (optional)

FIND IT IN:
The Endless Forest Feast (page 157)

PAIR IT WITH:
Tea Bag Broth (page 53), Golden Chicken Concentrate (page 64), Sesame Chile Crunch (page 123)

Mung bean, a very small and very delicious legume, is a beloved ingredient in Asian cooking, no doubt for its nutritive value, swift cooking time, and mild, faintly sweet flavor. In Chinese cuisine, mung beans, often called "green beans" or ludou, are deftly incorporated into numerous sweet and savory preparations. They're worked into a sticky paste for molded mooncakes, pureed into ice pops or refreshing drinks, sprouted and then cooked into stir-fries, thickened into congee or cooling dessert soups, or transformed into a starch to make wobbly jelly or bouncy cellophane noodles (sometimes called bean thread or glass noodles)—which also happen to be ideal for hot pot.

At home, nothing is easier, or more satisfying, than making a simple, super-nutritious meal by folding some cooked mung beans into fluffy, steamed rice. At the hot pot table, a pilaf is the perfect starchy accompaniment, ready to receive hot, bubbling soup. In that moment, the pilaf transforms into a uniquely soupy, starchy stew. Eat the pilaf with bites of cooked meat, seafood, tofu, and vegetables, and drizzle with additional dipping sauces (see page 116), if you like.

Soak the dried mung beans in a bowl of cold water for at least 1 hour and up to 8 hours.

Discard the soaking water and transfer the beans to a small pot. Add 1 cup (240 ml) of the filtered water. Bring to a boil over high heat, then reduce the heat to a very low simmer and cook until the beans are just tender, and not falling apart, 20 to 25 minutes, tasting for doneness along the way.

Let the beans rest in their cooking liquid until you are ready to make the pilaf. They can be cooked up to 2 days in advance and held in their cooking liquid in an airtight container in the refrigerator.

→

HOT (POT) TIPS

Look for dried whole mung beans at the grocery store, which look like teeny-tiny jelly beans and hold their shape after cooking. If split mung beans are all you can find, just be aware that they'll cook much more quickly and don't require presoaking—so start tasting early, and often.

The leftover bean cooking liquid can fortify any hot pot broth—simply use it in place of water.

Rinse the rice in a strainer with cold water until the water runs clear. Transfer the rice to a small pot and add the remaining 1 cup plus 2 tablespoons water (270 ml) and the salt. Bring to a simmer, then cover the pot, reduce the heat to very low, and gently cook the rice for 15 minutes. Remove from the heat and let the rice steam, covered, for 10 minutes.

Add the rice vinegar, toasted sesame oil, and soy sauce to the rice. Drain the mung beans and add those, too. Fold the mixture with a big spoon very gently so as to not break the rice or beans.

To serve, transfer the pilaf into a deep ramen-style bowl, patting the mixture down to compact it. Place a serving plate on top and swiftly invert the bowl. Gently wiggle and remove the bowl, revealing the molded pilaf. Decorate with fresh herbs, a whole tangerine, or dried goji berries, if desired.

Caramelized Mushroom and Cabbage Dumplings

MAKES ABOUT 45 TO 48 DUMPLINGS

1 cup (170 g) water chestnuts

1 bunch fresh cilantro

1 cup (50 g) roughly chopped Chinese chives or scallions

2 king oyster mushrooms, roughly chopped (about 5⅓ ounces/150 g)

One 3½-ounce (100 g) package maitake mushrooms

8 shiitake mushrooms, roughly chopped (about 2 cups/100 g)

2 cups (about 100 g) wood ear mushrooms

1 small napa cabbage, roughly chopped (just more than 1 pound/about 500 g)

2 tablespoons extra virgin olive oil

1 tablespoon sesame oil

1 teaspoon kosher salt

¼ teaspoon ground black pepper

¼ teaspoon ground white pepper (from about ½ teaspoon whole white peppercorns)

3 tablespoons Shaoxing wine

1 tablespoon fermented black bean sauce

INGREDIENTS CONTINUED →

Dumplings, or jiaozi, definitely don't need meat to be delicious. Mushrooms and cabbage are often relegated to supporting "filler" status in pork- or seafood-heavy dumplings, providing moisture, bulk, and balance to richer ingredients. Yet their naturally umami-forward characteristics make them delicious stars for a dumpling. A low, slow stovetop caramelization draws out the plentiful quantities of water from the raw vegetables, resulting in an intense, concentrated dumpling farce.

Place the water chestnuts, cilantro, and chives in the bowl of a food processor. Pulse until the water chestnuts and herbs are finely minced. Scrape out the mixture and transfer to a large bowl.

Add the king oyster, maitake, shiitake, and wood ear mushrooms to the food processor. Pulse until the mixture is a coarse rubble. Scrape out the mushrooms and transfer to a separate large bowl.

Add the napa cabbage to the food processor and pulse until a fine confetti forms. Scrape out the cabbage and add to the bowl of mushrooms.

Heat the olive oil and sesame oil in a large pan or pot over medium heat. Once the oil is shimmering, add the mushrooms and cabbage all at once and stir to coat in the oil. Cook, stirring occasionally, until the mixture has reduced by half, about 15 minutes.

Add the salt, black pepper, and white pepper to the pan. Reduce the heat to medium-low and cook for another 20 minutes, until the mixture looks caramelized and frizzled and is sticking to the pan in places.

→

1 teaspoon Sesame Chile Crunch (page 123), or a store-bought variety

1 teaspoon soy sauce

1 tablespoon minced garlic

2 teaspoons minced ginger

1 egg

1 package spinach-flavored round dumpling wrappers, chilled (about 50 pieces; thaw overnight in the refrigerator if frozen)

HOT (POT) TIP Some hot pot restaurants offer pan-fried dumplings as a crunchy, greasy appetizer to enjoy alongside the soup. For the perfect crispy-chewy dumpling, heat a tablespoon of vegetable oil in a wide, nonstick skillet over medium heat until shimmering. Add as many dumplings as will fit in the pan, so they fit snugly, and fry until the bottoms of the dumplings are deeply golden, 4 to 5 minutes. Slowly pour ⅓ cup (80 ml) of water into the pan and cover. Steam for 4 to 5 minutes, or until the water is mostly evaporated. Remove the lid and continue to cook until the pan is dry and sizzling once again, 1 minute longer. Serve immediately.

FIND IT IN:
The Endless Forest Feast (page 157)

PAIR IT WITH:
Tingly Beef Broth (page 59), Toasted Cumin and White Sesame Sauce (page 122)

Deglaze the pan with the Shaoxing wine, scraping up the flavorful burnt bits.

Add the fermented black beans, Sesame Chile Crunch, soy sauce, garlic, and ginger to the pan. Cook for a few minutes longer, then turn off the heat.

Let the mixture cool completely, about 30 minutes. Stir in the chopped water chestnuts, cilantro, and chives. Add the egg and mix until fully combined. You should have about 5 cups (850 g) of the vegetable mixture. This filling, stored in an airtight container in the refrigerator, can be made up to 2 days in advance of shaping the dumplings.

When you're ready to shape the dumplings, line a baking sheet with parchment paper. Fill a small bowl with water and pull the dumpling wrappers from the refrigerator.

The process of eyeballing the correct amount of filling and crimping the dumpling shut will improve with repetition; aim for 2 heaping teaspoons, or just shy of a tablespoon, and err on the side of underfilling the dumplings, so they don't burst in the soup.

Spoon the filling into the center of a dumpling wrapper. Dip a fingertip into the water and then run it around the edge of the wrapper. Fold the wrapper in half, pressing it closed at the top edge but leaving it open on each end.

To crimp the dumpling closed, keep the back half of the wrapper flat, and use your fingertips to tug the front half of the wrapper toward the apex, where it is already sealed, pressing the pleat against the back wall of the wrapper to seal it shut, for three pleats in each direction. Aim for six pleats total for a securely sealed dumpling (see opposite). Transfer the shaped dumpling to the lined baking sheet.

Repeat with the remaining wrappers and filling.

Freeze the dumplings on their baking sheet for about 1 hour, then transfer them to an airtight container and keep frozen until you are ready to eat.

At the hot pot table, set out a bowl of frozen dumplings. The dumplings will cook all the way through in simmering broth in 4 to 5 minutes.

Finding the Rhythm: Folding Dumplings Like a Pro

Once the filling is cooked, mixed, and seasoned, you'll begin the pleasant process of crimping the dumplings shut. Put on your favorite music. Sit somewhere comfortable. You'll appreciate these comforts for the repetitive movement, especially as you feel your hands grow nimbler and the stack of shaped dumplings builds.

Of course, there are simpler methods for trapping filling inside a thin slip of dough. If you don't want to deal with the pleats technique outlined here, take inspiration from my mom, who finds the fiddly finger movements uncomfortable and laborious. She simply moistens the edges of the wrapper with a dab of water, folds it over into a half moon, and firmly seals the edges shut, like a pierogi. Easy, fast—and just as delicious.

Scallop and Fish Roe Dumplings

MAKES ABOUT 20 DUMPLINGS

8 ounces (230 g) scallops, thawed if frozen, patted dry (about 6 large scallops)

2 ounces (60 g) bamboo tips

¼ cup (20 g) finely chopped chives

1 tablespoon Shaoxing wine

½ teaspoon minced ginger

½ teaspoon toasted sesame oil

¼ teaspoon ground white pepper (from about ½ teaspoon whole white peppercorns)

½ teaspoon kosher salt

2 tablespoons tobiko (flying fish roe), chilled

20 to 25 round dumpling wrappers, chilled (thaw overnight in the refrigerator if frozen)

FIND IT IN:
This Heat Feast (page 187)

PAIR IT WITH:
Cashew-Lime Salsa Macha (page 124)

Hand-shaped dumplings stuffed with delicate, sweet scallops are a luxurious addition to the hot pot table—and a much thriftier way to showcase special-occasion seafood. Scallops are a popular ingredient for steamed and boiled dumplings, especially in Cantonese-style dim sum. Here just a handful of scallops is stretched into almost two dozen dumplings, and they have a secret, sexy ingredient: a tiny scoop of crunchy, umami-rich tobiko, or flying fish roe, which pop in your mouth like briny sprinkles. A handful of tender bamboo tips, easily found at an Asian grocery store in refrigerated pouches or shelf-stable cans, echoes the delicate sweetness of the scallops.

Mince the scallops finely, like corn kernels. You should have about 1 cup.

Finely chop the bamboo tips; you should have about ⅓ cup.

Combine the scallops, bamboo tips, chives, Shaoxing wine, ginger, toasted sesame oil, white pepper, and salt in a large bowl. Stir gently to combine.

Line a baking sheet with parchment paper. Fill a small bowl with water and pull the dumpling wrappers from the refrigerator.

The process of eyeballing the correct amount of filling and crimping the dumpling shut will improve with repetition; aim for 2 heaping teaspoons, or just shy of a tablespoon, and err on the side of underfilling the dumplings so they don't burst in the soup.

Spoon the filling into the center of a dumpling wrapper. Add ¼ teaspoon of the tobiko on top of the filling. Dip a fingertip into the water and then run it around the edge of the wrapper. Fold the wrapper in half, pressing it closed at the top edge but leaving it open on each end.

HOT (POT) TIP

Since the prep is so elaborate, make more dumplings than you need for a single hot pot session. Start building that freezer dumpling bank now and thank yourself later—consider it a precious layaway for future hot pot parties.

To crimp the dumpling closed, keep the back half of the wrapper flat, and use your fingertips to tug the front half of the wrapper toward the apex, where it is already sealed, pressing the pleat against the back wall of the wrapper to seal it shut, for three pleats in each direction. Aim for six pleats total for a securely sealed dumpling (see page 93). Transfer the shaped dumpling to the lined baking sheet.

Repeat with the remaining wrappers and filling.

Freeze the dumplings on their baking sheet for at least 1 hour, then transfer them to an airtight container and keep frozen until you are ready to eat.

At the hot pot table, set out a bowl of frozen dumplings. The dumplings will cook all the way through in simmering broth in 4 to 5 minutes.

Shrimp and Pea Shoot Dumplings

MAKES 12 DUMPLINGS

- 3 cups (about 90 g) pea shoots
- 3 tablespoons finely chopped cilantro
- 1 teaspoon minced garlic
- 1 teaspoon minced ginger
- 1 teaspoon Shaoxing wine
- ½ teaspoon sesame oil
- ¼ teaspoon kosher salt
- ¼ teaspoon ground white pepper (from about ½ teaspoon whole white peppercorns)
- 12 medium shrimp peeled and deveined, preferably with the tails attached
- 12 round dumpling or square wonton wrappers, chilled (thaw overnight in the refrigerator if frozen)
- 1 tablespoon vegetable oil

FIND IT IN:
The Northern Classic Feast (page 67)

PAIR IT WITH:
Sesame Chile Crunch (page 123)

While at times I love a long, repetitive task—like chopping a slew of ingredients for dumplings—you *can* streamline the process. In lieu of spending time hunched over a cutting board, my mom has found a clever shortcut that results in a sculptural dumpling. Instead of a traditional fine mince, drape a single peeled shrimp, nestled into a bed of crunchy pea shoots, right into the dumpling wrapper, its tail fins dangling out. As the dumpling cooks, the wrapper hugs the contours of the shrimp like a gauzy slip. The effect is ethereal and dramatic; the bite is generous and rich. The aromatic pea shoots add freshness and balance, and the dumpling, lifted out of its hot pot bath, is as satisfying and sumptuous as any you'll encounter—and barely any chopping required.

Fill a bowl with ice cubes and water and set aside. Bring a small pot of water to a boil. Blanch the pea shoots in the boiling water for 15 seconds and then immediately plunge them into the ice bath.

Wring the excess water from the pea shoots; you should have about ⅓ cup.

Finely chop the pea shoots and transfer them to a medium bowl. Add the cilantro, garlic, ginger, Shaoxing wine, sesame oil, and half of the salt and white pepper. Stir to combine.

Pat the shrimp dry and sprinkle them with the remaining salt and white pepper.

Line a baking sheet with parchment paper. Fill a small bowl with water and pull the dumpling wrappers from the refrigerator.

Spoon a heaping ½ teaspoon of the pea shoot mixture into the center of a dumpling wrapper. Dip a fingertip

HOT (POT) TIP

A small, cylindrical fryer basket, with its offset handle and porous walls, is perfect for protecting delicate dumplings from the roiling hot pot broth. Look for a fryer basket at least 3 inches (7.5 cm) deep, so it can rest on the floor of the hot pot vessel while the dumplings dance inside.

into the water and run it around the edge of the wrapper. Place a shrimp on top of the filling. Fold the wrapper in half, pressing it closed all around, and sealing the opening where the tail pokes through, being sure to push out any air bubbles. Transfer the shaped dumpling to the lined baking sheet.

Repeat with the remaining wrappers and filling.

Freeze the dumplings on their baking sheet for about 1 hour, then transfer them to an airtight container and keep frozen until you are ready to eat.

At the hot pot table, set out a bowl of frozen dumplings. The dumplings will cook all the way through in the simmering broth in 3 to 4 minutes.

For crispy edges, boil the dumplings until cooked through, about 4 minutes (they should bob to the surface and float). Then remove with a slotted spoon and gently pat dry. Heat the vegetable oil in a large skillet over medium heat until shimmering. Add the dumplings and fry until they are lightly golden on the bottom, about 2 minutes. Serve immediately.

Garden Wontons

MAKES ABOUT 35 WONTONS

3 cups (200 g) finely chopped napa cabbage

1½ teaspoons kosher salt

1 bunch fresh scallions

½ bunch fresh cilantro

1 cup (35 g) Thai basil leaves, picked from the stem (about ½ bunch)

8 ounces (230 g) ground pork

1 tablespoon finely minced garlic

1 tablespoon finely minced ginger

2 teaspoons Shaoxing wine

1 teaspoon oyster sauce

1 teaspoon Sriracha chile sauce

¼ teaspoon ground black pepper

¼ teaspoon ground white pepper (from about ½ teaspoon whole white peppercorns)

30 shiso leaves or 15 perilla leaves

1 package (about 35 to 40) square wonton wrappers, chilled (thaw overnight in the refrigerator if frozen)

2 tablespoons vegetable oil

FIND IT IN:
The Land and the Sea Feast (page 105)

PAIR IT WITH:
Sticky Calamansi Vinaigrette (page 117); Royal Chrysanthemum Broth (page 57)

When it comes to composing the perfect dumpling filling, ratios are everything. Nothing beats a juicy pork dumpling, but I tend to think of meat as the foundation for lighter, more herbaceous ingredients to emerge. Ribbons of napa cabbage and a veritable mountain of fresh herbs like cilantro, scallions, and basil add a verdant liveliness and potent, aromatic flavor. (As a bonus, the bounty of greenery, woven throughout the pork, works as a net, preventing the farce from shrinking away from the wrapper as it cooks, a common issue in meat-heavy dumplings.) Don't forget the secret slip of fragrant shiso, a sheer layer in this dumpling garden.

Massage the chopped cabbage with ½ teaspoon of the salt in a large bowl. Let the cabbage sweat for 15 minutes while you prepare the rest of the filling.

Trim the scallions of their white bottoms, reserving them for making broth (like the Ginseng and Pork Bone Broth, page 61). Finely chop the green tops; you should have about 1 cup (70 g).

Finely chop the cilantro, including the stems; you should have about a heaping ½ cup.

Finely chop the Thai basil leaves; you should have about ½ cup.

Use your hands to squeeze any excess water from the cabbage, discarding the water. Add the scallions, cilantro, Thai basil, and ground pork to the bowl with the cabbage. It will look like too many green things, but that is the whole idea.

Add the remaining 1 teaspoon salt and the garlic, ginger, Shaoxing wine, oyster sauce, Sriracha, black pepper, and white pepper. Mix everything together well to create a smooth filling.

→

HOT (POT) TIPS

The very best way to determine if you want more heat, salt, or other seasonings is to cook a small amount of the filling first. Preheat a small skillet over medium heat. Add a little oil and then a tablespoon of the pork mixture, pressing it flat. Cook for 2 minutes on each side, let cool briefly, then taste.

Looking to keep your hot pot feast gluten-free? It's not uncommon to have a bowl of seasoned dumpling filling at the hot pot table. If you'd rather skip shaping the dumplings with wrappers, just set out a bowl of uncooked farce. Spoon tablespoon-sized meatballs and drop directly into the broth; they'll cook in just a few minutes.

When you're ready to shape the wontons, line a baking sheet with parchment paper. Fill a small bowl with water and pull the wrappers from the refrigerator.

Place one small shiso leaf (or a torn fragment of a larger perilla leaf) in the center of a wrapper. Place 1 tablespoon of filling on top of the leaf. Dip a fingertip into the water and then run it around the edge of the wrapper. Fold the wrapper in half diagonally, pressing the edges closed with your fingertips, forming a triangle.

Moisten the two points that form the line of the diagonal, then pull them together so they touch. Pinch them together to seal, forming the wonton shape. Transfer the shaped wonton to the lined baking sheet.

Repeat with the remaining wrappers and filling.

Freeze the wontons on their baking sheet for about 1 hour, then transfer them to an airtight container and keep frozen until you are ready to eat.

At the hot pot table, set out a bowl of frozen wontons. The wontons will cook all the way through in the simmering broth in 4 to 5 minutes.

For crispy bottoms, boil the wontons until cooked through, 4 to 5 minutes, then remove with a slotted spoon, shaking off the excess water. Heat the vegetable oil in a large skillet over medium heat. Add the wontons and fry until golden brown on the bottom, about 4 minutes. Serve immediately.

Seal the Deal: Tidy Presents Packed with Flavor

You'll need square wonton wrappers to achieve this neat envelope shape, which come together faster than pleated dumplings. A strategically placed flag of a bright, wide herb like perilla or shiso (basil or mint would be lovely as well) adds a secret pop of flavor, too.

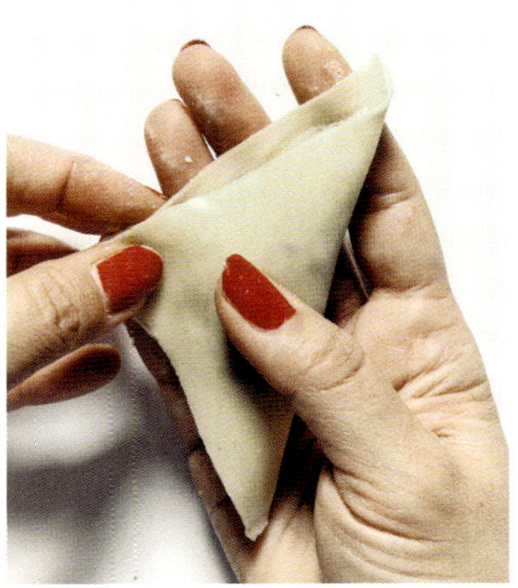
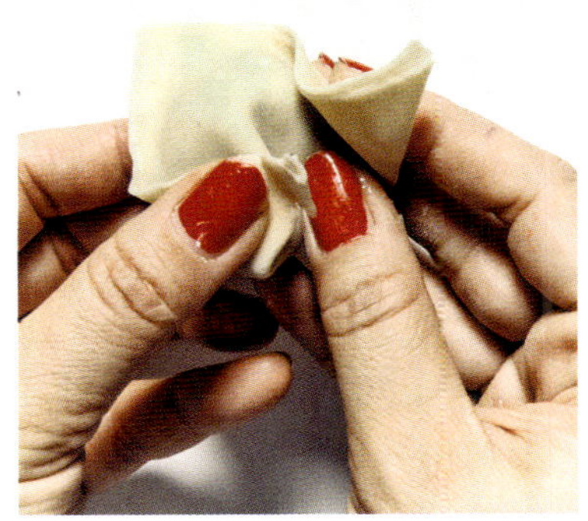

The Land and the Sea

Though hot pot is a natural framework for budget-strapped dining, there's a time and place to pull out all the stops. When cost is no object, hot pot is a glorious opportunity to convey abundance, especially in a themed surf-and-turf dinner. Don't hold back—in addition to a bevy of tempting ingredients, you'll also set out a DIY sauce bar on a side table or counter, allowing your guests full access to the profusion of condiments and sauces.

You'll arrange a medley of chilled seafood on chipped ice alongside platters of sliced beef, flanked by artful skewers and hand-shaped dumplings. And don't forget the pièce de résistance: a bonus raw bar—packed with roe, oysters, and sashimi—for a full range of textures, temperatures, and flavors.

If you love a dramatic tablescape, this is your dream menu. Garnish platters with edible flowers and tendrils of herbs. Pull out those seafood platters and cake stands (and find more table setting tips on page 43). This is pure theater—and expect a chorus of oohs and aahs.

HOT (POT) TIP

There's nothing like slurping down freshly shucked, ice-cold oysters alongside all the traditional hot pot offerings. Garnish them with a splash of Black and Brown Vinegar (page 116) or Sesame Chile Crunch (page 123).

GET READY

Review your equipment and ingredient checklists before grocery shopping, including whatever variety of ingredients you'd like to try for the sauce bar (see page 128). If you can, wait until the day of the feast to buy all the fresh seafood, keeping it cold until the hot pot begins. Asian grocery stores usually have a stellar, varied seafood selection—and more competitive prices than Western groceries when it comes to specialty items like trays of uni, jars of roe, or fresh oysters and clams.

HOT (POT) TIP

Get creative with your table setting strategy. With so many ingredients on tap, it's not uncommon for the main hot pot table to be flanked by ancillary surfaces, where the ingredients spill out onto extra spaces. Children's play furniture, folding card tables, stools, and ottomans all do the trick.

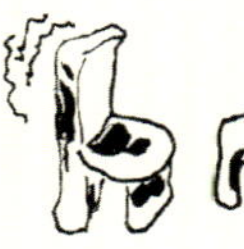

Check the freezers for flash-frozen high-end ingredients, like king crab legs and lobster claws. For your raw bar offerings, your local fishmonger will have the best of fresh, regional varieties like mackerel, yellowfin, halibut, cuttlefish, or scallops; always look for signs that explicitly state they are wild-caught, sustainable, or sashimi-grade and buy whatever looks freshest and best.

The day before the party, make the Kombu Brown Butter (page 86) for the Texas toast, keeping it chilled until you're ready to serve. Mix the filling and shape the Garden Wontons (page 101), storing them in the freezer. Cook the Ginseng and Pork Bone Broth (page 61), so the maximum flavor is extracted from the bones overnight.

The day of the party, whip up the Mushroom Dashi (page 50), which comes together in minutes. Assemble all the skewers, keeping them chilled and wrapped until the meal begins, and prep and plate the rest of the ingredients. Whisk together the Black and Brown Vinegar (page 116). Assemble the Crunchy Seaweed Boats (page 152) and the Perfect Fruit Plate (page 184) shortly before guests arrive. Ask friends to bring wine—you'll be glad to have it off your to-do list.

THE TABLESIDE STRATEGY

Before you begin, ask everyone to make a trip to the sauce buffet, where they'll create their own unique dipping sauce. The joy of this banquet is all about contrast: alternating hot bites with cold ones, or delicately poached seafood with melt-in-your-mouth Wagyu beef. Once everyone is sufficiently stuffed, you'll bring out a ceremonial fruit platter for the final round of feasting.

THE MENU

EQUIPMENT LIST (see page 18)

KNIFE CUTS AND COOKING INSTRUCTIONS (see page 27)

RUN OF SHOW (see page 40)

THE BROTHS

Mushroom Dashi (page 50)

Ginseng and Pork Bone Broth (page 61)

THE SAUCES

Sauce bar (see page 128)

Black and Brown Vinegar (page 116)

THE STARCHES

Kombu and Brown Butter Texas Toast (page 86)

Garden Wontons (page 101)

THE SALAD

Crunchy Seaweed Boats (page 152)

THE DRINKS

1 bottle chilled, sparkling wine, ideally Champagne from growers like Suenen or Cedric Bouchard

1 bottle light-bodied, chilled red wine, like a Gamay from the Loire (see Annie Shi's wine recommendations on page 206)

1 bottle baijiu, like Ming River (see Resources, page 214)

THE DESSERT

The Perfect Fruit Plate (page 184)

THE SPREAD

8 shrimp and kale skewers (page 39)

8 bay scallop and fava bean skewers (page 39)

8 enoki and Wagyu skewers (page 39)

4 ounces (115 g) whole clams, scrubbed clean

4 ounces (115 g) king crab legs

8 ounces (226 g) sliced rib eye steak

4 ounces (115 g) tofu skin rolls

4 ounces (115 g) bok choy

4 ounces (115 g) celtuce, sliced thinly

1 bunch dark greens (about 12 ounces/340 g; choose from The Hot Pot Ingredient Guide, page 29)

1 bunch fresh scallions, sliced

1 bunch fresh cilantro, chopped

BONUS RAW BAR

4 ounces (115 g) tuna sashimi

4 ounces (115 g) salmon sashimi

4 ounces (115 g) salmon roe, sturgeon caviar, or flying fish roe (tobiko)

12 oysters, on the half shell

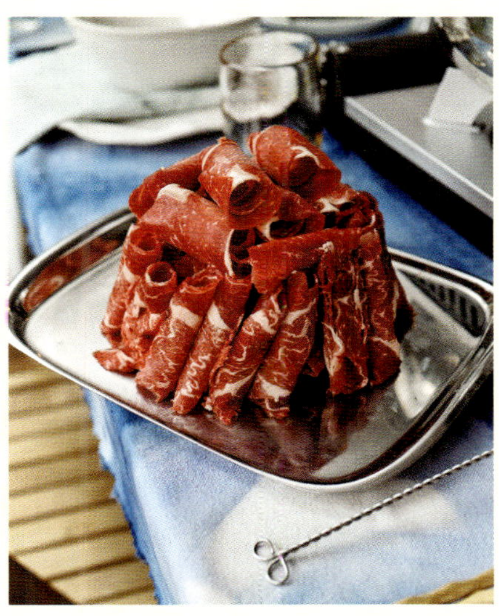

HOT (POT) TIP

A feast this luxurious deserves a bottle of good baijiu (see page 212). A night of both hot pot and baijiu can feel like an endurance test—especially when it comes to downing shots, which is the traditional way to drink this liquor (it's rarely just sipped). Baijiu is a social drink, and it is considered impolite to drink on your own. Toasting is the best way to bring the table together, but the host (you!) should always be the first to start. If you're a guest, it's a sign of respect to always keep the rim of your glass lower than that of all the others. Sometimes this can result in a mad clash of wills to see who can reach the table—or even the floor—first.

SAUCES &

BBQ
SAUCE POT
HOT
SOUP
BASE
FOR
HOT POT
SESAME OIL
SPIRITS
SESAME

SEASONINGS

Bold Hot Pot Enhancements

Sauce is what takes hot pot beyond the realm of soup, and into something ineffably grand and distinctive. You simply can't have hot pot without it. The technique is intuitive: Briefly blanch a small bite in bubbling broth, then dunk it in an intense dipping sauce. In this process of building layers of flavor, the sauce adds richness to otherwise lean bites. Over the course of the meal, the cycle of dipping enriches both the broth *and* the dipping sauce, climaxing in a final bowl of nourishing soup—a unique by-product of a long hot pot session.

My mom serves only one dipping sauce—a creamy, nutty sludge made with white sesame paste and fermented bean curd—and ladles it directly into our soup bowls. This typically northern Chinese sauce remains the cornerstone of my own sauce offerings; you'll find it incorporated in the Northern Classic Feast (page 67).

But there are a variety of different sauces, vinaigrettes, and oils that add explosive flavor to any hot pot table. Think about how black vinegar can lift softened eggplant (see page 140), how a crimson chile oil coats thin slips of mushroom (see page 155), how flecks of candied citrus play with poached shrimp. Here you'll find an assortment of delicious sauces that riff on popular Chinese condiments, like chile crunch (page 123), a classic dumpling sauce (page 116), and my cumin-speckled version of my mom's famous sesame sauce (page 122).

Making sauces from scratch means you are in charge. Though there are many store-bought jarred and bagged sauces, they're often loaded with preservatives, sodium, and bad-for-the-environment oils. Once you've built out your dream hot pot pantry (see Resources, page 214), you'll have everything you need to make a memorable, lip-smacking sauce in a matter of minutes. Ideally, you'll choose a duet of sauces—one adding bright acidity, the other a fatty richness—to your hot pot table.

The recipes are scaled to serve a hot pot party of four—but you'd be prudent to make big batches of your favorites to use on everything from breakfast tacos to big, crunchy salads to late-night noodles.

Chinese Celery Salt

MAKES ½ CUP (87 g)

1 bunch Chinese celery (about 10½ ounces/300 g)

½ cup (80 g) kosher salt

Citric acid

FIND IT IN:
Hot Pot Bouillon (page 48)

PAIR IT WITH:
Crunchy Seaweed Boats (page 152), sliced lamb, scallops, sweet potato

If you've ever thought that celery was too mild or bland, then get to an Asian grocery right away and try Chinese celery—it's Western-style celery turned up to 100. The crisp stalks tend to be thinner, and there are more of the leafy tops, which exude a powerful savory fragrance. The leaves are low in moisture and dry out in a pan easily; once toasted, they're an assertive savory note for seasoning broths, sauces, dumpling filling—really, anything you want.

Pluck 2 loosely packed cups (about 40 g) of leaves from the celery stalks. (Save the stalks for broth or a crunchy salad, page 146.)

Set a wide skillet over low heat. Place the leaves in the skillet and gently toast until they are crisp but not browned. Stir occasionally while the leaves shrink down; depending on the size of the leaves and the level of heat, this will take between 20 and 25 minutes. Let the leaves cool completely.

Once toasted, the leaves should reduce to about 1 cup (7 g), packed. Transfer the leaves to a blender and pulse until fine. Transfer them to a small jar and stir in the salt. Add a small pinch of citric acid.

Store the salt in an airtight container at room temperature for up to 2 months.

Black and Brown Vinegar

MAKES 1 CUP (240 ml), ENOUGH FOR 4 SERVINGS

½ cup (120 ml) black vinegar

2 tablespoons dark brown sugar

2 tablespoons soy sauce

¼ cup (about 15 g) thinly sliced ginger, for garnish

¼ cup (8 g) finely chopped cilantro stems, for garnish

FIND IT IN:
The Land and the Sea Feast (page 105)

PAIR IT WITH:
Garden Wontons (page 101), sliced pork belly

Chinkiang vinegar, a type of Chinese black vinegar made with fermented rice, has a malty, caramelized tang that you'll immediately want to pour all over steamed dumplings, pan-fried noodles, and flaky fish. Black vinegar is less acidic than a Western-style vinegar, but what it does have is a rich, inky undercurrent of earthiness and musk that truly transforms the simplest dish.

Similar to a classic dumpling dipping sauce, in this recipe black vinegar is balanced with a bit of seasoning, by way of soy sauce and brown sugar. The final flurry of chopped cilantro stems and julienned ginger adds a weightless, fresh brightness.

Combine the black vinegar, brown sugar, and soy sauce in a small bowl and whisk together. When you're ready to serve, top with the ginger and cilantro stems.

Serve immediately, or transfer to an airtight container and store in the refrigerator for up to 1 week. Add the cilantro stems and ginger right before serving.

Sticky Calamansi Vinaigrette

MAKES ⅔ CUP (230 ml), ENOUGH FOR 4 SERVINGS

½ cup (180 g) honey

2 teaspoons ground gochugaru chile flakes

2 tablespoons calamansi juice or lime, yuzu, or tangerine juice

2 teaspoons powdered Chinese hot mustard

2 teaspoons rice vinegar

2 teaspoons sesame oil

2 teaspoons soy sauce

Prickly heat, a relaxed sweetness, and sneaky acidity—this vinaigrette provides sharp contrast to anything that emerges from a bubbling hot pot. There's a squeeze of juice from calamansi, a small, sour citrus similar to a tangerine and kumquat, but wholly itself. (While it's tricky to find the fresh fruit unless you live in a sunny region where the trees grow, frozen packets of calamansi juice are readily found in Asian grocery stores like H Mart; see Resources, page 214.) There's a spoonful of Chinese hot mustard powder, which clears the sinuses like horseradish or wasabi but tastes entirely different. (You've probably squeezed a packet on deep-fried egg rolls, where it cuts through fat like a blade.) A spoonful of vinaigrette goes a long way—try it in tandem with something more mellow and rich, like the Toasted Cumin and White Sesame Sauce (page 122).

FIND IT IN:
The Endless Forest Feast (page 157)

PAIR IT WITH:
Sliced chicken breast, cubed halibut, Not-Just-Scallion Pancakes (page 83)

Pour the honey into a small pot and bring to a boil over medium-high heat. Remove from the heat, add the gochugaru, and swirl to infuse. Pour into a small heatproof bowl.

Add the calamansi juice, powdered hot mustard, rice vinegar, sesame oil, and soy sauce and whisk until smooth.

Transfer the vinaigrette to an airtight container and store in the refrigerator for up to 1 week.

HELLO HOME

Tableside Tips: Making Sense of the Chaos

IF YOU'RE SOMEONE who craves structure, rules, and order, you may find the open-ended, meandering, swelling rhythms of hot pot unnerving. Though I don't believe in hard-and-fast rules for having a great hot pot experience, there are plenty of strategies I've picked up along the way that will lead you to hot pot success.

Protect your outfit. Many hot pot restaurants provide giant garbage bags for safeguarding coats and purses from the powerful scent of cooked onions or fryer oil settling into the fibers of your favorite outerwear. At home, be sure to check everyone's coats into a side room, or, if you live in a studio apartment like me, a tied-up garbage bag will work just as well. A tiny ziplock baggie for everyone's cell phone is a good idea, too (which also deters your guests from using their phones too much!).

The splatter is real. In the back-and-forth rhythms of hauling slippery noodles and runny sauces from the hot pot to your face, it's inevitable that your shirt may end up splattered with food. Some hot pot restaurants provide bibs or even an apron to wear at the table; at home, you can offer the same, with either disposable lobster bibs or pretty linen napkins to be tucked into your guests' tops.

Ventilate. My parents believe that hot pot *really* gets going once the windows turn damp with steam and condensation, but a little fresh air keeps everyone more comfortable. If you're burning butane, be mindful of ventilation—keep a window open, a fan blowing off to the side, or a hood range on.

Streamline the table. When it comes to hot pot, it's common for more dishes to appear on the table than you'd see at a Thanksgiving feast. I make room for the bounty—and prevent any accidents caused by arms reaching across the table—by keeping the lit candles and flower arrangements off to the side, and not at the main table. (Or if you can't resist a moody taper candle or two, use them to set the ambience while guests arrive—then move them to the side when you're ready to sit.)

Add support. Small side tables, card tables, or a low folding table can "extend" your dining room table by providing extra surface area for ingredients, a common tactic employed by hot pot restaurants. Store overflow—like pitchers of drinks, backup platters of ingredients, and clusters of condiments and sauces—off to the side.

Charred and Candied Orange Sauce

MAKES 1½ CUPS (420 g), ENOUGH FOR 4 TO 6 SERVINGS

1 medium orange, such as navel

2 cups (480 ml) filtered water

1 cup (240 ml) fresh orange juice (from about 5 small oranges or 3 navel oranges)

½ cup (100 g) sugar

3 tablespoons rice vinegar

2 tablespoons soy sauce

1 tablespoon minced garlic

1 tablespoon minced ginger

Choose Your Fighter (*from top*): *Black and Brown Vinegar, Charred and Candied Orange Sauce, Toasted Cumin and White Sesame Sauce, Sticky Calamansi Vinaigrette*

FIND IT IN:
This Heat Feast (page 187)

PAIR IT WITH:
Thinly sliced beef, cauliflower, squid, Shrimp and Pea Shoot Dumplings (page 99)

This sweet-and-sour sauce is a bit like the beginning of making a marmalade—the peel, first charred in a hot pan, is blanched and then softly candied in syrup. The final aromatics are whisked in, and the sauce transforms into a glossy, sticky gel, thanks to the natural pectin in the cooked orange peel.

Heat a medium pot over medium heat. Slice the orange in half and place both halves cut side down in the pot. Let them char, uncovered, until the edges of the peel are blackened, 5 to 8 minutes.

Remove the orange halves from the pot and cool. Peel them; you should have 1 cup (90 g) of torn peel.

Juice the peeled, charred fruit with clean hands (it should yield about ⅓ cup/70 ml) and set aside.

Pour the filtered water into the pot you used to char the orange (no need to wash the pot). Add the orange peel. Simmer until the skin is tender and the pith is translucent, about 10 minutes. Remove the peel and discard the water.

Add the reserved charred orange juice, along with the fresh orange juice and sugar, to the pot and bring to a simmer. Add the orange peel and cook until the peel is candied and sheer, about 15 minutes.

Remove the pot from the heat. Add the rice vinegar, soy sauce, garlic, and ginger and stir to combine. Using an immersion blender or a food processor, blend the sauce until the orange peel pieces are like chunky confetti. The sauce should be viscous and glossy; it will continue to thicken as it cools.

Let cool completely, then transfer to an airtight container and store in the refrigerator for up to 2 weeks.

Toasted Cumin and White Sesame Sauce

MAKES ABOUT 2¼ CUPS (500 ml), ENOUGH FOR 6 SERVINGS

2 teaspoons cumin seeds

½ cup (130 g) Chinese white sesame paste

¼ cup (60 ml) shacha sauce

¼ cup (60 ml) rice vinegar

¼ cup (65 g) fermented tofu chunks, in their sauce

2 tablespoons minced garlic

2 tablespoons minced ginger

2 tablespoons toasted sesame oil

1 tablespoon soy sauce

½ cup (120 ml) filtered water

¼ cup (8 g) chopped cilantro leaves, for garnish

My mom's white sesame sauce is the one I most closely associate with hot pot. I insist newcomers try it first, because I know they'll fall in love right away.

The secret ingredient is fermented tofu (see page 69), which melts into the sauce, leaving behind a fruity whiff redolent of sour cherries, pineapple, and tangerines. Shacha sauce (or "Chinese barbecue sauce"), a thick, grainy paste made with everything from dried shrimp to crushed shallots, is another nonnegotiable flavor booster.

Though you could substitute tahini for the Asian sesame paste, the results won't be quite as toasty tasting, as Chinese sesame paste uses ground roasted unhulled seeds. If the sesame paste has a layer of water on top, invert the jar overnight, or at least for 3 hours, to allow it to blend gradually.

Toast the cumin seeds in a small pan over low heat, about 3 minutes. Set aside to cool.

Combine the sesame paste, shacha sauce, rice vinegar, fermented tofu, garlic, ginger, sesame oil, and soy sauce in a medium bowl and whisk together. The mixture will be very thick, similar to stiff peanut butter.

Gradually add the water, 1 tablespoon at a time, while whisking, until the mixture lightens in color and has the consistency of a whipped milkshake. You may not need the full ½ cup (120 ml) of water.

Transfer the sauce to an airtight container and store in the refrigerator for up to 1 week.

At the hot pot table, ladle ⅓ cup (80 ml) of the sauce into small soup bowls, refreshing throughout the night as needed. Top with a sprinkle of the toasted cumin seeds and chopped cilantro.

FIND IT IN:
The Northern Classic Feast (page 67)

PAIR IT WITH:
Napa cabbage, sliced leg of lamb, lotus root, glass noodles

Sesame Chile Crunch

MAKES 1½ CUPS (380 g), ENOUGH FOR 6 SERVINGS

1 cup (240 ml) vegetable oil

¼ cup (24 g) ground gochugaru chile flakes

1 tablespoon Sichuan peppercorns, coarsely ground

1 tablespoon dark brown sugar

2 teaspoons kosher salt

1 teaspoon ground cumin

¼ cup (30 g) roasted white sesame seeds

2 tablespoons roasted garlic

2 tablespoons dried shallot

1 tablespoon toasted sesame oil

I've tried just about every brand of chile crisp out there, but I'll always prefer this homemade version. It's a blast to make—the sizzling oil! The intoxicating scent! And cooking it from scratch allows you to control the quality of the ingredients, the level of heat, and, crucially, the ratio of oil to crunchy add-ins. And this condiment is all ASMR crunch, with just enough oil to bind it all together.

Skip frying fresh shallot and garlic, which can quickly burn and taste bitter in the oil, and opt instead for store-bought dried chips and morsels. Similarly, you'll want Japanese-style roasted sesame seeds, or iri goma, which stay crispy in the hot oil. This crunch won't melt your face off, but that's not the point; the ample aromatics are just as important as the smoky-sweet heat of the chiles. Look for ground gochugaru, which adds a floral, moderate heat and dyes the oil a brilliant crimson.

Pour the vegetable oil into a small pot and place over medium-low heat.

Combine the gochugaru, Sichuan peppercorns, brown sugar, salt, and cumin in a medium heatproof bowl.

After the oil has been heating for about 5 minutes, flick a drop of water into it to test the temperature. If the oil is hot, it will sizzle and hiss. Once it is ready, slowly pour the oil over the seasonings. (The mixture will sputter and pop; be careful and stand back!) The mixture should smell nutty and sweet, like buttered toast or movie theater popcorn.

Stir the mixture and set aside to cool completely, about 1 hour.

Add the roasted sesame seeds, roasted garlic, dried shallot, and sesame oil and stir to combine.

Transfer the mixture to an airtight container and store in the refrigerator for up to 1 month.

FIND IT IN:
The Endless Forest Feast (page 157)

PAIR IT WITH:
Vermicelli noodles, clams, mung bean sprouts

Cashew-Lime Salsa Macha

MAKES 1½ CUPS (400 g), ENOUGH FOR 4 TO 6 SERVINGS

1 cup (240 ml) vegetable oil

1 cup (130 g) raw cashews

6 garlic cloves, peeled

1 cup (30 g) dried Sichuan chiles

2 tablespoons minced ginger

¼ cup (24 g) ground gochugaru or Aleppo chile flakes

¼ cup (60 ml) fresh lime juice

2 teaspoons soy sauce

2 teaspoons sugar, plus more to taste

½ teaspoon kosher salt, plus more to taste

FIND IT IN:
This Heat Feast (page 187)

PAIR IT WITH:
Caramelized Mushroom and Cabbage Dumplings (page 91), enoki mushrooms, firm tofu

Salsa macha, a Mexican chile oil typically made with ground-up bits of nuts, seeds, dried chiles, and herbs, has a lot in common with complex Asian condiments like sambal oelek and chile crisp, and it absolutely belongs on your hot pot table. Here buttery cashews are fried in oil, along with an intense mix of chiles and fresh aromatics, before being ground up into a thick, pebbly paste. Rich, glossy condiments are essential to adding weight and substance to a bowl of soup—and this salsa macha can be stirred right into a basic broth (see page 64); spooned on top of blanched greens, meats, and seafood; or used in concert with other flavor-building blocks at your sauce bar (see page 128). Don't let the chiles deter you—the sauce is only moderately spicy.

Be sure to have all of your ingredients prepped and ready before heating the oil; the procedure moves quickly once the oil is at temperature.

Pour the vegetable oil into a medium pot and place over medium-low heat. After the oil has been heating for about 5 minutes, flick a drop of water into it to test the temperature. If the oil is hot, it will sizzle and hiss.

Add the cashews and fry until golden, stirring occasionally, 4 to 5 minutes. Remove with a slotted spoon and place in a heatproof bowl.

Add the garlic cloves to the pot and fry until golden brown, stirring continuously, 1 to 2 minutes. Remove with a slotted spoon and add to the bowl.

Add the dried Sichuan chiles to the pot and fry briefly, stirring continuously, about 1 minute. (Blackened chiles will make the oil taste bitter.) Remove with a slotted spoon and add to the bowl.

Turn the heat off, add the ginger and chile flakes to the pot, and stir. (If the ginger is very juicy, stand back a bit in case the oil sputters.)

Pour the hot oil mixture over the cashew mixture and stir to combine. Stir in the lime juice and soy sauce.

Let the mixture cool until it is just warm to the touch, about 30 minutes. Then transfer to the bowl of a food processor or blender and process the mixture until it is chunky but not a fine puree.

Taste, then add the sugar and salt. Taste again; the macha should be well seasoned but not salty. Add more sugar and salt if needed.

Store the salsa macha in an airtight container in the refrigerator for up to 1 month.

Some Like It Hot (*from left*): *Sesame Chile Crunch, Cashew-Lime Salsa Macha*

Lighting and operating instructions
1. Open canister cover. 2. Turn the knob to OFF position and place the
fuel canister with the canister guidein the up right position. 3. Push
down the canister fix lever to the FUEL LOCK position. 4. Turn the knob
to the IGNITION position until ignition device makes a clear click sound.
5. To turn off, return the knob to the OFF position. 6. Return the canister
This portable gas stove shall be used with 227g
fuel gas canister UL listed to 147B and meets all applicable DOT
regulations for canisters and cartons.

A Little of Everything: Building Your Dream Sauce Bar

WHILE IT'S IMPORTANT to have some tried-and-true dipping sauce recipes in your repertoire, the convivial, do-it-yourself ethos of hot pot can extend to your sauce strategy. After all, everyone knows that the most crowded station at any hot pot restaurant is the sauce bar buffet, where diners build their own signature dipping sauce as gleefully as kids spooning sprinkles and hot fudge onto ice cream sundaes.

A great dipping sauce blends sweet, savory, sour, rich, funky, and umami elements. Advise your fellow diners to begin with a small spoonful of a raw aromatic (like minced garlic, chopped scallions, or sliced ginger) and a big dollop of something fatty and rich (like sesame paste or peanut butter), tempered by a sharp acid (like rice vinegar or lemon juice) and a funky ferment (like preserved black beans or leek flowers), and with just enough salt (like soy sauce or oyster sauce) to make it taste mouthwatering.

As an extension of the hot pot tablescape, individual condiments can be portioned into small ramekins, bowls, or squeeze bottles (and tiny spoons and small tongs are useful for lifting pastes or fresh herbs from narrow-necked jars or dishes). When you have a smaller group, you can leave the various condiments, greasy bottles, and half-empty jars just as they are, clustered together on the table or a nearby counter. Hot pot isn't precious, and your sauce setup doesn't have to be, either.

Select at least two items from each category for the kind of mouthwatering versatility that will improve any kind of broth or scenario you can imagine. Slide batches of your favorite from-scratch sauces next to the store-bought items.

RAW, FRESH AROMATICS
(Pick 3)

- ☐ Celery, finely diced
- ☐ Chives, minced
- ☐ Cilantro, chopped
- ☐ Garlic, chopped
- ☐ Ginger, minced or finely sliced
- ☐ Hot peppers, like bird's-eye chile or jalapeño, finely sliced
- ☐ Scallions, chopped

PANTRY-STABLE SEASONING
(Pick 3 or 4)

- ☐ Chinese Celery Salt (page 115)
- ☐ Dark brown sugar
- ☐ Flaky sea salt
- ☐ Fried garlic (sometimes sold as "dried garlic")
- ☐ Fried shallots (sometimes sold as "dried shallots")
- ☐ Fried soybeans
- ☐ Ground black pepper
- ☐ Ground Sichuan peppercorns
- ☐ Ground white pepper
- ☐ MSG
- ☐ Red pepper flakes
- ☐ Roasted peanuts, chopped
- ☐ Seaweed flakes
- ☐ Toasted white sesame seeds

THICK AND CREAMY EMULSIFIERS AND FATS
(Pick 1 or 2)

- ☐ Almond butter
- ☐ Black sesame paste
- ☐ Brown butter
- ☐ Extra virgin olive oil
- ☐ Hazelnut oil
- ☐ Neutral-tasting oil (like avocado or grapeseed)
- ☐ Raw egg yolk
- ☐ Smooth peanut butter
- ☐ Toasted Cumin and White Sesame Sauce (page 122)
- ☐ Toasted sesame oil
- ☐ White sesame paste

TART JUICES, VINEGARS, AND WINES
(Pick 2)

- ☐ Apple cider vinegar
- ☐ Black and Brown Vinegar (page 116)
- ☐ Charred and Candied Orange Sauce (page 121)
- ☐ Chinese black vinegar
- ☐ Chopped kumquats
- ☐ Fresh lemon and lime wedges
- ☐ Rice vinegar
- ☐ Shaoxing wine
- ☐ Sticky Calamansi Vinaigrette (page 117)
- ☐ White wine vinegar
- ☐ Yuzu juice

SOUR, SWEET, AND FUNKY FERMENTS AND PICKLES
(Pick 1 or 2)

- ☐ Black bean sauce
- ☐ Cabbage or radish kimchi
- ☐ Chinese pickled garlic
- ☐ Fermented bean curd
- ☐ Leek flower sauce
- ☐ Pickled mustard greens or cabbage
- ☐ Spicy bean paste

SPICY SAUCES, OILS, AND PASTES
(Pick 1 or 2)

- ☐ Calabrian chile “bomba” sauce
- ☐ Cashew-Lime Salsa Macha (page 124)
- ☐ Chile oil
- ☐ Chile paste
- ☐ Gochujang
- ☐ Sambal oelek
- ☐ Sesame Chile Crunch (page 123)
- ☐ Sriracha chile sauce
- ☐ Yuzu kosho

SAVORY, UMAMI-RICH CONDIMENTS
(Pick 2)

- ☐ Fermented soybean paste (like miso or doenjang)
- ☐ Fish sauce
- ☐ Hoisin sauce
- ☐ Liquid aminos
- ☐ Oyster sauce
- ☐ Shacha sauce
- ☐ Soy sauce
- ☐ Tamari
- ☐ XO sauce

韮花醬
LEEK SAUCE
REFRIGERATE AFTER OPENING ⇨OPEN⇨
BLACK BEAN
豆豉
NET WT:380g(13.4oz)
台灣製造 MADE IN TAIWAN
明德
SINCE 1950
芝麻醬
Sesame Sauce
TO OPEN ➡
weichuan
柚子こしょう
TASTING NOTES
Nutrition Facts

GENUINE BREWED
E VINEGAR
SINCE 1941
TAIWAN
CHINKIANG VINE
YUZUCO
100% YUZU JUICE
低塩
だし醤油
LESS SODIUM DASHI SOY SAUCE
SESAME CHILI CR
CASHEW SALSA MACHA
TART
SALAD · SOUP
VINEGAR
沙茶醬
THAI
KITCHEN
fish sauce

SALADS

SNACKS

Crisp & Cool Complements

Elaborate Chinese meals, with their dizzying kaleidoscope of textures, ingredients, techniques, and flavors, are a masterful study of balance and harmony. For every sour dish, there might be something bitter or sweet. For every crunchy mouthful, a slick of something sticky. The table isn't cluttered—it's intentional. And the more Chinese feasts you participate in, the more you will notice and appreciate the effort made to create these harmonious relationships.

Nowhere is this effortless balance expressed more vividly than at the hot pot table. After all, the cooking vessel itself—traditionally divided into two equal, mutually perpetuating chambers—is often shaped like the swirling yin and yang symbol, which emphasizes how opposite forces not only are interconnected but also structurally support and enhance each other. This philosophy extends beyond the hot pot object itself and wends its way into all other modes of culinary expression, including the auxiliary bites that accent the main hot pot feast.

A proper hot pot spread isn't just about the soup and its accompanying raw ingredients; you'll also find a concise selection of appetite-whetting snacks meant to complement the meal. At home, you'll want to keep the appetizer part of the meal simple. In addition to a variety of your favorite store-bought xiao chi, or small snacks (try roasted peanuts, shrimp chips, garlicky dried broad beans, and spicy peas), offer a selection of crunchy, pungent pickles and salads, which won't fill up your guests but rather pique the appetite for the impending feast.

The dressings are light, minimal, acidic, and bright. The vegetables are crunchy and snappy, ethereal and herbal, saturated and coiffed. These dishes can be enjoyed as an amuse-bouche before hot pot begins or as a cooling, crisp reprieve, mingling on the hot pot table alongside everything else. They are part of the rhythm of hot pot—a sip of soup, a slip of blanched cabbage, a crunch of pickle, a glug of beer—and play an essential role in the greater balance of the meal.

Chile Crisp Snack Mix

MAKES 8 CUPS (600 g); SERVES 6 TO 8

2 cups (70 g) woven rice cereal, like Chex

2 cups (55 g) shrimp chips (look for the Calbee brand)

2 cups (100 g) fried wonton strips

1 cup (55 g) small cheese crackers, like Cheez-Its

1 cup (130 g) roasted, unsalted peanuts

4 tablespoons (½ stick/55 g) unsalted butter

¼ cup (57 g) Sesame Chile Crunch (page 123), or a store-bought variety

2 tablespoons sweet chili sauce

2 tablespoons black vinegar

½ tablespoon soy sauce

3 tablespoons dried wakame seaweed

2 tablespoons untoasted white or black sesame seeds

You don't just jump into hot pot—it's imperative to ease into the meal with a round of cold drinks and crunchy snacks. An informal cocktail hour gives people a chance to relax and chat before the very serious business of hot pot begins. If you, like me, have trouble choosing just one or two snacks from the store, then this snack mix, an irresistible mélange of the best treats from the grocery store snack aisle, is the ultimate recipe. The snacks, dunked in a buttery, spicy bath, are baked low and slow in the oven until fragrant and bronzed. Substitutions work well here; play around with your own favorite crackers, nuts, seeds, and cereals, keeping the volume measurements the same. The Sesame Chile Crunch (page 123) really brings it all together, so don't skimp.

Preheat the oven to 275°F (135°C). Line a half baking sheet with parchment paper.

Combine the rice cereal, shrimp chips, wonton strips, cheese crackers, and peanuts in a large bowl.

Melt the butter in a small pot over low heat. Add the Sesame Chile Crunch, sweet chili sauce, black vinegar, and soy sauce and whisk until smooth and emulsified. Add the wakame and sesame seeds and stir until the seaweed is rehydrated and soft, 2 to 3 minutes.

Pour this mixture over the dry snacks and toss well to combine. Spread into one layer on the lined baking sheet and transfer to the oven.

Bake for 35 to 45 minutes, stirring occasionally, to allow the mix to dry out and gently toast until it is darkened in places and there are no damp spots; the mixture will continue to crisp up as it cools. Do not overbake! Remove from the oven and let cool completely.

Store the snack mix in an airtight container at room temperature for up to 1 month.

FIND IT IN:
The Northern Classic Feast (page 67)

PAIR IT WITH:
Cold beer, Al's Baijiu Punch (page 211)

Never-Ending Pickles

MAKES 1 QUART (950 ml) OF PICKLES IN THEIR BRINE

1 medium beet, peeled

1 large carrot, peeled

½ lotus root segment, peeled

½ daikon radish (about the size of an orange), peeled

One 1-inch (2.5 cm) piece ginger

4 garlic cloves, peeled

4 Thai chiles (or similar, such as 1 jalapeño or 1 serrano pepper)

½ cup (120 ml) rice vinegar or distilled white vinegar

½ cup (120 ml) soy sauce

½ cup (120 ml) filtered water

¼ cup (50 g) dark brown sugar

HOT (POT) TIP Intensify any hot pot broth with a spoonful of the leftover brine.

FIND IT IN:
The Endless Forest Feast (page 157)

PAIR IT WITH:
Mung Bean and Rice Pilaf (page 89)

Pickles are an unimpeachable introduction to any rich meal; the pungent soy sauce brine makes quick work of a variety of produce, which should be sliced very thinly to promote quick and even pickling.

Pickling brines begin with some blend of salt, sugar, acid, and water, but from there the improvisations are endless. Here we emphasize the richly caramel essence of both soy sauce and brown sugar, spike it with the sweet kiss of Thai chiles, and finish with fresh aromatics. Look for a rainbow's worth of crunchy root vegetables, like radish, carrot, beet, and lotus root, but truly, you could find pickle happiness in cucumber, onion, cauliflower, and turnips, too, as long as they're sliced thinly.

Slice the beet, carrot, lotus root, and radish very thinly into coins about as thick as a nickel (a Japanese mandoline will do this quickly and consistently). Each pickle should be bite-size, or no bigger than a potato chip.

Slice the ginger into ¼-inch-thick (0.6 cm) rounds. Smash the garlic cloves with the back of your knife or the bottom of a glass. Slice the chiles in half lengthwise. (For a less spicy brine, leave the chiles whole.)

Pack the sliced vegetables into a 1-quart (950 ml) heatproof jar, distributing the garlic cloves, ginger slices, and chile halves evenly throughout.

Combine the rice vinegar, soy sauce, water, and brown sugar in a small pot. Bring the mixture to a simmer, stir to dissolve the sugar, and remove from the heat.

Pour the hot brine into the jar stuffed with sliced vegetables. The vegetables should be just about submerged (and they'll release a considerable amount of water as they pickle).

Let the jar cool completely, then chill for at least 2 hours. Store the pickles in the refrigerator for up to 2 weeks.

NEVER ENDING PICKLES

Thai Basil and Eggplant Agrodolce

MAKES 1½ CUPS (300 g); SERVES 4

2 dried jujubes

1 cup (240 ml) filtered water

2 teaspoons cornstarch

3 tablespoons black vinegar

3 tablespoons maple syrup

2 tablespoons soy sauce

1 tablespoon plus 1 teaspoon Sriracha or a similar chile sauce

1 tablespoon oyster sauce

1 medium Chinese eggplant (about 7 ounces/200 g)

½ teaspoon kosher salt

¼ teaspoon ground white pepper (from about ½ teaspoon whole white peppercorns)

1 tablespoon plus 1 teaspoon olive oil

1 tablespoon minced ginger

2 teaspoons minced garlic

1 Thai chile, sliced thinly

¼ cup (7 g) Thai basil leaves, picked from the stem

FIND IT IN:
The Endless Forest Feast (page 157)

PAIR IT WITH:
Kombu and Brown Butter Texas Toast (page 86), glass noodles, firm tofu, sliced king trumpet mushrooms

Agrodolce is a delicious, sticky Italian condiment made by cooking down eggplant in vinegar and sugar until it is tacky and soft. It bears more than a passing kinship to traditional Chinese preparations of eggplant, which also lean into sweet-and-sour notes.

When shopping, look for Chinese eggplant, which should be slightly bendy, with even, purple skin. This variety is less watery than the plumper Western-style eggplant, and cooks to a mild sweetness that pairs beautifully with aromatics and strong black vinegar.

Place the dried jujubes in a small bowl. Pour the water into a small pot or teakettle, bring to a boil over high heat, and pour over the jujubes. Set aside and allow the jujubes to soften and relax.

Combine 1 teaspoon of the cornstarch with the black vinegar, maple syrup, soy sauce, Sriracha, and oyster sauce in a small bowl. Whisk together and set aside.

Slice the eggplant in half lengthwise, then cut those halves in half lengthwise, so you have four long strips. Cube each strip into pieces about 1 inch (2.5 cm) wide. Transfer to a colander, resting in the sink, and toss with the salt. Let drain for 10 minutes.

Remove the softened jujubes from the hot water and coarsely chop them into chunky pieces, discarding the seeds. Set aside.

Pat the eggplant dry. Sprinkle the remaining 1 teaspoon cornstarch and the white pepper all over and toss to coat.

Warm a medium pan over medium heat, then pour in 1 tablespoon of the olive oil. Add the seasoned eggplant. Deeply brown the eggplant on all sides, letting it fry untouched for several minutes before stirring, 7 to 8 minutes total. Transfer the eggplant to a small bowl.

Add the remaining 1 teaspoon olive oil to the pan, followed by the ginger, garlic, and Thai chile. Reduce the heat to low and gently fry for about 30 seconds, moving the aromatics around continuously.

Pour the black vinegar mixture into the pan. Stir to combine and allow the mixture to reduce until syrupy, 30 seconds.

Turn off the heat and add the jujubes and eggplant. Stir to coat evenly, then fold in the Thai basil.

Store the agrodolce in an airtight container in the refrigerator for up to 1 week.

Asian Pear, Jicama, and Fennel Slaw

SERVES 4

2 tablespoons fresh lime juice (from about 2 limes)

1 tablespoon white sesame paste

2 teaspoons soy sauce

1 teaspoon agave syrup or honey

½ teaspoon minced ginger

Pinch of ground white pepper (from about 5 whole white peppercorns)

1 Asian pear (about 8½ ounces/240 g)

½ jicama, scrubbed and peeled (about 5⅓ ounces/150 g)

½ fennel bulb (about 4¼ ounces/120 g)

1 teaspoon roasted white sesame seeds

1 tablespoon edible flowers, like borage or calendula (optional)

PAIR IT WITH:
Poached scallops, shrimp

Soft, chewy, and tender textures run abundant in hot pot, so it's a good idea to add something to the table that stands in sharp contrast. Crunchy, refreshing, raw, and light is always the way to go. Here you'll chop Asian pear, jicama, and fennel into batons, toss them into a bowl, and drizzle a creamy, nutty dressing on top.

"Asian" pear is a catch-all name to describe the mostly globe-shaped, thin-skinned, mild-tasting crunchy pears that are prized throughout East Asia. Look for Korean varieties, like the yellow pear, or the Chinese white pear, or ya pear.

To make the vinaigrette, combine the lime juice, white sesame paste, soy sauce, agave syrup, ginger, and white pepper in a small bowl. Whisk well and taste; the dressing should be tart and nutty and bright. Set aside.

Cut the pear in half lengthwise and then cut those pieces in half lengthwise, yielding four pieces. Remove the core by slicing into the pear pieces at an angle, then cut the pieces into slices about ⅓ inch (1 cm) wide. Cut those slices into matchsticks, also ⅓ inch (1 cm) wide.

Slice the jicama crosswise into ⅓-inch-thick (1 cm) rounds, then cut those into sticks about ⅓ inch (1 cm) wide.

Slice the fennel lengthwise into thin spears. (If you're making this salad in advance, you can keep the prepped produce in a large bowl filled with ice cubes and water, for up to 2 hours before plating.)

Spread the pieces out in a shallow bowl and spoon the dressing all over. Sprinkle the roasted sesame seeds on top and edible flowers, if using. Eat immediately.

Chinese Not-Quite-Pasta Salad

SERVES 4

1 cup (about 150 g) corn kernels, fresh or frozen

2 Chinese celery stalks

Three 10 by 7-inch (25 by 18 cm) squares of soy tofu sheets (150 g)

¼ cup (60 ml) rice vinegar

¼ cup (60 ml) avocado or grapeseed oil

2 tablespoons fresh lemon juice

2 tablespoons white miso paste

1 teaspoon grated ginger

¼ teaspoon kosher salt

1 tablespoon roasted white sesame seeds

Handful of cilantro leaves

Soy tofu sheets, which often come sold in stacks of ten sheets or more, like tidy, delicious reams of paper, are one of bean curd's most versatile incarnations. You can eat them cold, right out of the package, or griddle them over high heat for crispy, caramelized edges. Here the protein-rich, mild-tasting sheets are sliced into long, skinny noodles and tossed with crunchy nubs of corn and celery. Like your favorite pasta salad, the tangled threads thirstily drink up vinegars and oil—no cooking required.

Bring a small pot of water to a boil. Add the corn kernels and blanch for 1 minute. Drain well and set aside.

Slice the leafy tops off the celery and reserve them for a garnish. Slice the ribs in half lengthwise, then chop into a fine dice. You should have about ½ cup (38 g) of diced celery.

Roll the soy tofu sheets into a tight cigar, then slice into noodles about a scant ¼ inch (0.6 cm) wide, like linguine. Open the noodles with your fingers and arrange them into a loose nest shape, about 5 inches (13 cm) wide, right on a serving plate.

In the valley of the nest, spoon little piles of the blanched corn and diced celery.

To make the vinaigrette, combine the rice vinegar, oil, lemon juice, white miso paste, ginger, and salt in a small bowl and whisk together. Pour all over the noodles and vegetables.

Sprinkle the roasted sesame seeds all over the noodles, and garnish with the reserved celery leaves and cilantro. Serve immediately.

PAIR IT WITH:
Golden Chicken Concentrate (page 64), Sesame Chile Crunch (page 123)

Glorious, Shapeshifting Bean Curd: The Modest MVP of Hot Pot

BEAN CURD IS TRULY a miracle food—and hot pot wouldn't be the same without it. Over thousands of years, artisans and chefs have mastered the art of transforming this culinary chameleon into everything from meat to seafood to dairy to wheat.

Unfortunately, there are no standardized English translations for most Asian ingredients, especially the myriad iterations of soy products. It's common to come across similar products with slight variations in their names, which can be confusing when you're trying to check items off a grocery list. After all, untangling the semantic differences between soy tofu sheets, bean curd sheets, tofu skins, bean curd skins, tofu wrappers, yuba tofu, or soybean skins is enough to make anyone's head spin—and a lack of standardization speaks to a Western market resistance to give these ingredients household names, which would make them more accessible to every kind of shopper.

When shopping, you'll notice certain nuances. Bean curd sheets, or skins, are slightly sheer, rumpled, and natural-looking in texture, and they are made with the flavorful film that comes from cooking soy milk. (You may also know this product as yuba.) Typically, bean curd sheets are used for layering and stuffing with fillings, as in dim sum. Soy tofu sheets, which we use in the Chinese Not-Quite-Pasta Salad (page 146), are thicker and more closely resemble the mouthfeel of cooked, bouncy noodles, and they often have a mechanically uniform appearance or are stamped all over.

Calories
Total Fat
Sodium
Total Carb.
Protein

Cucumber and Peanut Pyramids

SERVES 4

4 Persian cucumbers

2 teaspoons kosher salt

2 garlic cloves, peeled

2 tablespoons rice vinegar

1 tablespoon soy sauce

1 teaspoon hot soybean paste

Pinch of sugar

⅓ cup (50 g) roasted Chinese peanuts (see Tip)

8 shiso or perilla leaves

HOT (POT) TIP

Sample a peanut before assembling the salad; if you'd prefer a louder crunch, dry roast the peanuts in a wide skillet over medium heat for 6 to 7 minutes, shaking the pan occasionally, until they look slightly blistered and are super-fragrant. Let cool completely, then proceed with the recipe as written.

FIND IT IN:
The Northern Classic Feast (page 67)

PAIR IT WITH:
Cashew-Lime Salsa Macha (page 124)

In a perfect world, every feast would begin with two small, appetite-whetting ingredients: raw, intensely seasoned cucumbers and crunchy Chinese roasted peanuts. At the restaurant chain Din Tai Fung, a fantastically popular Taiwanese export, the cucumbers arrive as chunky, bite-size stumps, stacked into a miniature pyramid. It's a beautiful dish—and, of course, extremely delicious. This salad takes great advantage of the Persian cucumber, a small, crisp variety with tender skin and non-slimy seeds. Spiky doilies of fresh shiso leaves weave in and out of the cucumbers, and their sweetness tones down the raw garlic and fermented soy. Flanking the pyramid is a ring of peanuts, swaddled in dressing.

Slice the cucumbers crosswise into 1-inch-tall (2.5 cm) stumps and transfer them to a medium bowl. Toss the rounds with the salt and let sit for about 15 minutes, while you prepare the vinaigrette. (The release of water will make the cucumber even crunchier.)

Grate the garlic into a fine paste using a Microplane or mortar and pestle and transfer it to a large bowl. Add the rice vinegar, soy sauce, hot soybean paste, and a pinch of sugar and mix.

Rinse the cucumbers and pat dry. Toss the cucumbers and peanuts in the bowl of dressing.

To serve, place four shiso leaves on a plate. Arrange half of the cucumbers on the plate, like tree stumps, in a tight oval. Add two more leaves on top, and another layer of cucumbers. Continue stacking the leaves and cucumbers until a rough pyramid shape is achieved. Spoon the peanuts around the perimeter. Drizzle any remaining dressing all over, and eat immediately.

Crunchy Seaweed Boats

SERVES 4

¼ cup (10 g) dried wakame or hijiki seaweed

2 tablespoons rice vinegar

1 tablespoon light soy sauce

1 teaspoon hot soybean paste

1 teaspoon toasted sesame oil

1 cup (100 g) coarsely grated carrot (about 1 large carrot)

¼ cup (20 g) scallion greens, sliced thinly into matchsticks

1 tablespoon roasted white sesame seeds

Kosher salt (optional)

1 head purple endive or Little Gem lettuce (about 4¼ ounces/120 g)

2 squares dried nori, sliced into matchsticks

FIND IT IN:
The Land and the Sea Feast (page 105)

PAIR IT WITH:
Black and White Shaobing (page 79)

Did you know that *all* seaweed is edible? Naturally, it's omnipresent in hot pot, whether flecked into a creamy compound butter (see page 86), steeped into a nourishing broth (see page 53), or twisted into chewy knots (see page 37), and it's extra delicious (and sneakily substantial) in this salad that makes absolutely everything taste better.

Play around with different varieties of seaweed to get a bouncy, crisp mixture of texture, thickness, and color. Wakame and hijiki, with their soft, translucent frills, are easy to find at the grocery store, where they're shredded into bite-size pieces. The bright, nutty dressing doubles as a hot pot dipping sauce. Even better, marinated seaweed only improves with an extra day or two in the refrigerator—just wait until the moment of serving to spoon the seaweed into the lettuce boats and top with crisp matchsticks of nori.

Place the seaweed in a bowl and cover with cold water. Let sit for a few minutes, or until softened and slippery, while you make the salad dressing.

Combine the rice vinegar, soy sauce, hot soybean paste, and toasted sesame oil in a medium bowl and whisk together.

Drain the seaweed, pressing out any lingering water, and add it to the bowl, along with the grated carrot and sliced scallions.

Toss well, add the roasted sesame seeds, toss again, and taste. Add a pinch of salt, if it needs it.

Let the salad sit for 15 minutes, so the seaweed can soak up the dressing. Pull the endive or lettuce into individual petals and arrange on a wide platter. Spoon about 2 tablespoons of the seaweed mixture into each upturned petal, and sprinkle the nori matchsticks on top. Eat immediately.

Spicy Wood Ear Mushrooms

SERVES 4

3 tablespoons Sesame Chile Crunch (page 123), or a store-bought variety

2 teaspoons soy sauce

1 cup (75 g) fresh wood ear mushrooms (see Tip)

¼ cup (8 g) roughly chopped cilantro

1 tablespoon rice vinegar

2 teaspoons fresh lemon juice

HOT (POT) TIP

Dried wood ear mushrooms are a perfectly worthy substitute for fresh; reconstitute them first in 2 cups (480 ml) of boiling water, plus a green tea bag for added flavor. Let sit for 15 minutes, then drain and pat dry. (Save the leftover mushroom tea to top off any hot pot broth.)

FIND IT IN:
This Heat Feast (page 187)

PAIR IT WITH:
Shrimp and Pea Shoot Dumplings (page 99), sliced beef tenderloin

If you see fresh wood ear mushrooms at the grocery store, buy them. Their springy, crunchy-yet-jellied texture is a deeply addictive and *very* Chinese ingredient, used in everything from soups to braises to salads. Their undulating, frilly folds are also highly absorbent, which makes them ideal as a marinated salad—enjoy them chilled or poached, briefly dunking each in a bubbling hot pot broth. Just sneak them onto your next hot pot table, where they'll hang out among all the other platters of ingredients—this batch makes enough for a few succulent bites for all.

Set a small pan over medium-low heat. Combine the Sesame Chile Crunch and soy sauce in the pan and swirl until the aromatics are faintly sizzling, about 3 minutes.

Remove the pan from the heat and immediately stir in the wood ear mushrooms, turning them to coat evenly. Add the cilantro, rice vinegar, and lemon juice and toss.

Serve chilled or at room temperature or dunk the marinated mushrooms in a hot pot broth to warm through.

Store the mushrooms in an airtight container in the refrigerator for up to 3 days.

The Endless Forest

Contrary to most Western mindsets, there is a cathartic pleasure to be had in enjoying hot soup on a hot day. Hot soup is deeply appreciated year-round all over Asia, especially in major cities that experience long, humid summers. Informal hot pot restaurants spring up in residential districts, with building exteriors lined with low tables and squat plastic stools, and crowded with people chatting over billowing pots of soup and cold beer.

One of the great pleasures of the hot pot meal resides in the customization and versatility of the ingredients you choose to include—and warmer seasons offer infinitely more local produce options than the cooler months. Trust me: Indulging in hot pot during peak summer will change everything you think you know about this meal.

TYNA'S TIP

After washing and processing greens and herbs, continue their spa day with a soak in an ice bath to keep them crisp and perky. For hot pot, simply shake off excess water before plating. There's no need to fully dry them as their next move is into the soup!

I find myself craving hot pot during our most explosive growing months of late summer and early fall. This is the time to visit your favorite farmers for impossibly gorgeous and flavorful vegetables—flounced bundles of greens, flowering herbs like chives and cilantro, fat heirloom tomatoes, pearly ears of corn, taut lobes of eggplant, peppers, and squash—before plunging them into a fragrant, lemongrass-spiked broth. Oh, and this menu just happens to be vegan, too.

If you can, serve this meal outdoors; it will blow your mind.

HOT (POT) TIP

Take inspiration from my mom, who loves to use tangerines as unexpected place cards. Write your guests' names right onto the peel; they'll get to eat the fruit, too.

GET READY

The day before, mix the dipping sauces and let rest overnight. Chop up the watermelon and freeze for the slushies. Freeze the banana slices and raspberries for the ice cream. Cook the Charred Tomato and Lemongrass Broth (page 54) and Tea Bag Broth (page 53) and let rest overnight (you can also make and freeze them up to 2 weeks in advance; pull them out now to thaw). Finally, prepare the filling for the Caramelized Mushroom and Cabbage Dumplings (page 91).

The day of the party, boil the mung beans until tender and steam the rice for the pilaf (see page 89). Shape the dumplings (see page 92) and freeze them until you're ready to eat.

At least 3 hours before the party, puree the frozen banana slices and raspberries with the rest of the ingredients for the Raspberry and Coconut Ice Cream (page 172) and freeze again. When your guests arrive, blitz the frozen watermelon for the Watermelon Shiso Slushies (page 205).

When the hot pot meal is winding down, puree the frozen cubes of ice cream a final time, then scoop and serve.

THE TABLESIDE STRATEGY

On a scorching hot day, you'll want to keep all your ingredients as cold as possible until the last possible moment, and definitely keep everyone's thirst quenched with plenty of beverages on hand. Small handheld electric fans provide relief to sticky, hot faces, as do prechilled face towels layered with ice cubes. Citronella, a natural bug repellent, is in the same family as lemongrass. Its sweet, citrusy fragrance complements the hot pot feast; look for long-burning candles or incense to form a protective ring around your guests. The added smoke, mingling with the steam, creates an intoxicating atmosphere your guests won't soon forget.

HOT (POT) TIP

With more casual, alfresco feasts, go heavy on the handheld items—and prebuilt skewers are the best way to show off fancy seasonal produce. Choose any three skewers from the options shown on page 39, or make up your own combination, to add even more interactive fun to the meal.

THE MENU

EQUIPMENT LIST (see page 18)

KNIFE CUTS AND COOKING INSTRUCTIONS (see page 27)

RUN OF SHOW (see page 40)

THE BROTHS

2 quarts (1.9 L) Charred Tomato and Lemongrass Broth (page 54)

2 quarts (1.9 L) Tea Bag Broth (page 53)

THE SAUCES

Sticky Calamansi Vinaigrette (page 117)

Sesame Chile Crunch (page 123)

THE STARCHES

Caramelized Mushroom and Cabbage Dumplings (page 91)

Mung Bean and Rice Pilaf (page 89)

THE SALADS

Thai Basil and Eggplant Agrodolce (page 140)

Never-Ending Pickles (page 138)

HOT (POT) TIPS

If you can't find fresh mushrooms, substitute with their dried counterparts. Soak the dried mushrooms in hot water for at least 10 minutes, or until they feel soft and pliable. Then proceed with the recipe as written.

My friend Leanne Gan, an artist and expert hot pot practitioner, likes to keep a small pitcher of soy milk on the table to augment her vegan broth bases. It's so refreshing and cooling—you'll love it, too.

THE DRINK

Watermelon Shiso Slushie (page 205)

THE DESSERT

Raspberry and Coconut Ice Cream (page 172)

THE SPREAD

12 ounces (340 g) kelp noodles, or similar

4 ounces (115 g) firm tofu, cubed into 1-inch (2.5 cm) pieces

4 ounces (115 g) smoked tofu, sliced into thin slabs

4 ounces (115 g) tofu skin rolls

4 ounces (115 g) maitake mushrooms, torn into bite-size pieces

4 ounces (115 g) lion's mane mushrooms (or similar; see page 32), torn into bite-size pieces

4 ounces (115 g) brown beech mushrooms (or similar; see page 32)

2 ears corn, shucked and cut into quarters (200 g)

3 heads Little Gem lettuce, halved

1 pint (280 g) cherry tomatoes

1 pint (280 g) long beans or green beans

½ bunch fresh cilantro

½ bunch Thai basil

½ bunch purple shiso

1 avocado, cubed

¼ bunch Swiss chard, torn into palm-size pieces

¼ bunch chrysanthemum greens

3 limes, quartered

Edible flowers, for garnish

DESSERTS

A Not-Too-Sweet Finale

Dessert may not be the main attraction at a hot pot feast, but it's a critical part of the dining narrative and should not be ignored, skipped, or dismissed. These days, showier hot pot restaurants place just as much focus on an array of elaborate desserts—snowy mountains of shaved ice capped with condensed milk and adzuki beans, serve-yourself matcha and black sesame soft serve, made-to-order skewers of rock sugar–dipped fruit, bowls of ice jelly made with the seeds of the Awkeotsang fig—but at home, dessert can, and should, be quite uncomplicated.

A not-too-sweet dish is a delicate, palate-cleansing epilogue. It can be as simple as a bowl of ice cream, sliced fruit, or a tray of your favorite store-bought cookies or candies, served with a pot of tea or something a little naughtier, like sherry or huangjiu (Chinese yellow wine).

Of course, there will be moments when you'll feel compelled to present something from scratch—and these recipes will barely make a dent in your prep lists. You won't turn your oven on to make these desserts; you won't need a stand mixer or any high-tech equipment, either. While there's a time and place for an opulent layer cake or custardy dessert, you'll be so sated after hot pot, broth swishing in your belly, that you'll long for something buoyant and simple.

Fruit is the answer, whether chopped into a tart granita (see page 169), frozen into a creamy ice cream (see page 172), coated with a crisp sugar shell (see page 177), sliced into wobbly jelly (see page 167), or steamed and stuffed with crunchy soy nuts (see page 183). A fruit plate is an iconic finale to any Chinese feast, and the presentations can range from the opulent to the unfussy. For more insights from the chef whose friends call him a "fruit sommelier," don't miss advice from Tristan Kwong, a man with an infamous fruit plate reputation (see page 184).

Double Mango Jelly

SERVES 4

1¼ cups (300 ml) filtered water, gently warmed

2 tablespoons (20 g) powdered gelatin or 8 silver-strength gelatin sheets

1 lime

1½ cups (about 230 g) mango chunks, fresh or thawed from frozen

¼ cup (50 g) sugar

Pinch of kosher salt

Pinch of citric acid (optional)

1 fresh mango

FIND IT IN:
The Northern Classic Feast (page 67)

PAIR IT WITH:
Bouquet Tea (page 198)

Even if you're full beyond measure, it's difficult to leave the dinner table without a *little* bit of something. It could be a small bite of something sweet, like a cookie, or refreshing, like a crisp pear, or elucidating, like a strong tea. It's a coda that signals that the meal has truly concluded. The Chinese have mastered the art of that simple moment of closure, and one of my favorite desserts—especially when I'm too full for a slice of cake or scoop of ice cream—is a gelatinous mango-flavored domino, served matter-of-factly on a small disposable plate, at many casual Chinese canteens in New York City. At home, an additional slip of fresh mango is a welcome textural surprise, and all in all, an elegant and low-key way to wrap things up.

Measure ¼ cup (60 ml) of the warm water into a shallow, wide bowl and sprinkle the gelatin powder on top, then let sit for 5 minutes to bloom. (If using gelatin sheets, soften them in a bowl of ice water for at least 5 minutes.)

Zest the lime; you should get about 1 teaspoon's worth. Juice the lime; you should get 2 to 3 teaspoons' worth.

Puree the lime juice, lime zest, and mango chunks in a blender until smooth. Measure out 1 cup (230 g) of the puree and pour into a medium bowl.

Set a small pot over low heat. Add the sugar and the remaining 1 cup (240 ml) water and stir until the sugar dissolves and the syrup is hot but not simmering. Turn off the heat and whisk in the bloomed gelatin gel. (If using gelatin sheets, wring out the excess water from the sheets, add them to the hot syrup, and whisk until fully dissolved.)

Stream the syrup into the mango puree and whisk well to combine. Strain the mixture through a fine-mesh sieve. Taste. Add a small pinch of salt and, if you like, a small

HOT (POT) TIP

For an extra flourish, top the jelly dish with a drizzle of condensed milk, a sprinkle of flaky sea salt, and a teaspoon of toasted black sesame seeds.

pinch of citric acid, which helps the mango taste vibrant and bright.

Line an 8 by 4-inch (20 by 10 cm) loaf pan with plastic wrap. Pour the mango mixture into the pan and refrigerate, uncovered, until set, at least 3 hours.

When the jelly has firmed up completely, remove from the fridge and invert the pan onto a cutting board. Peel back the plastic wrap. Portion the jelly into bars about ½ inch (1.3 cm) wide and 2 inches (5 cm) long.

When you're ready to serve, portion the fresh mango: Slice off each side, being careful not to hit the long, flat seed. With the cut side facing up, score the two mango pieces vertically, making cuts about ½ inch (1.3 cm) apart. Scoop out the slices with a big spoon.

Drape slices of the fresh mango onto the slices of the mango jelly. For an extra-neat look, trim the mango into 2-inch-long (5 cm) bars to match the length of the jelly, pressing them to adhere to the jelly. Eat immediately; the jellies, tightly wrapped and refrigerated, are best within 3 days.

Honey Tangerine Granita

SERVES 4

5 honey tangerines

¼ cup (60 ml) fresh lemon, lime, or calamansi juice (see Tips)

¼ cup (50 g) sugar

¼ cup (60 ml) filtered water

HOT (POT) TIPS

For an easy shortcut, look for freshly squeezed tangerine juice at the grocery store (Natalie's Orchid Island Juice Company makes my favorite store-bought version).

Calamansi juice is a fragrant, sour substitute for lemon juice. Look for frozen calamansi juice in the freezer aisles in Asian grocery stores, where it is often sold in 1-tablespoon packets.

FIND IT IN:

This Heat Feast (page 187)

PAIR IT WITH:

Double Mango Jelly (page 167), Baijiu Shooters (page 208)

Tangerines are an omnipresent component of any social gathering at my family's home, from long meals to house visits to late-morning tea. My lifelong love for citrus has become a cornerstone of my pastry chef practice, and over the years I've used the fruits in many of my dishes, always returning to the tangerine as my very favorite. A sparkling granita—a frozen syrup that's been scraped and fluffed into melt-in-your-mouth ice crystals—is one of the purest (and easiest) ways of conveying the immediacy of fresh fruit, especially citrus. The key is to taste and adjust the syrup before it is frozen, so you can control its mouth-twisting acidity.

At the grocery store, look for honey tangerines, which possess a thin rind loosely attached to the flesh, making them easy to peel and convert into serving vessels. Even better, in the winter months, most Asian groceries sell honey tangerines with the stem and leaf attached—a sweet little hat to cap a refreshing dessert.

Zest 1 tangerine, then remove and discard the rest of the peel. Set the zest and peeled fruit aside.

Using a small serrated knife, score the peel of the remaining 4 tangerines in half widthwise. With a tug of the finger, the top peel should release easily, all in one piece. Use your fingertips to pry the fruit out of each bottom peel.

Transfer the 4 tangerine-peel "bowls" to the freezer, until you're ready to serve. Reserve the top-peel "hats" at room temperature, to use as a garnish.

Juice the 4 peeled tangerines, straining out any seeds. You should have between 1 and 1⅓ cups (240 and 320 ml) of fresh juice. Stir in the lemon juice and the reserved tangerine zest, and set aside.

→

HOT (POT) TIP

For a tasty Creamsicle-esque variation, add a spoonful of vanilla ice cream or coconut sorbet to the bottom of the tangerine bowl, then top with granita. For a sophisticated, cocktail-inspired variation, replace the lemon juice with ¼ cup (60 ml) of dry white vermouth, or pour 1 ounce (30 ml) of the Baijiu Shooter (page 208) over the granita right before serving.

To make a simple syrup, combine the sugar and water in a small pot over low heat. Once the sugar has melted, remove the pot from the heat and let cool completely.

Add ¼ cup (82 g) of the cooled simple syrup to the tangerine juice mixture. Stir and taste. The syrup should be bright and sour and sweet, all at once. Add more syrup, 1 teaspoon at a time, until the balance is reached; you may not need all of the simple syrup.

Pour the mixture into a casserole dish or loaf pan (or any container in which the syrup will be about ¼ inch/0.6 cm in depth) and transfer to the freezer. Scrape the mixture every hour, pressing with the back of a fork to break up lumps of ice, until fluffy, 2 to 3 hours.

When you're ready to serve, slice the reserved fifth peeled tangerine into tiny pieces, about the size of hazelnuts.

Divide the granita evenly into the 4 frozen tangerine-peel bowls. Scatter the fresh tangerine pieces on top. Finish with the peel hats and serve immediately.

Raspberry and Coconut Ice Cream

SERVES 4

2 cups (about 300 g) banana chunks, frozen (from about 3 medium bananas)

1 pint (about 170 g) raspberries, frozen

¼ cup (60 ml) unsweetened, full-fat coconut milk

1 tablespoon fresh lemon juice

1 teaspoon vanilla extract

Kosher salt

Citric acid

2 tablespoons Raspberry Dust (recipe follows)

½ cup (70 g) fresh raspberries, for garnish

FIND IT IN:
The Endless Forest Feast (page 157)

At most all-you-can-eat hot pot restaurants, there isn't a formal dessert menu. Instead, you might get a complimentary dessert, like a swirl of soft serve in flavors like green tea, ube, mandarin, or black sesame. It's a very soothing, refreshing finish. To re-create that magic at home, all you need is a food processor to make dreamy, fruit-forward ice cream.

Place the frozen banana chunks in the bowl of a food processor. Process to a puree, 2 to 3 minutes. Add the frozen raspberries, coconut milk, lemon juice, vanilla, a big pinch of salt, and a small pinch of citric acid. Blend to combine.

Taste the mixture and adjust any seasonings, if desired. (The citric acid helps to both balance the sweet custard as well as preserve the color of the fresh fruit.)

Transfer the mixture to the compartments of a large ice cube tray and freeze for at least 1 hour and up to 1 week.

When you're ready to serve, place 4 small dessert bowls in the freezer. Twist the frozen ice cream cubes out of the ice cube tray and into the food processor. Buzz the cubes until the mixture is creamy, about 2 minutes.

Divide among the bowls, top with Raspberry Dust, and scatter fresh raspberries all over. Eat immediately.

Raspberry Dust

MAKES A HEAPING ½ CUP (70 G)

½ cup (60 g) toasted black sesame seeds

½ cup (10 g) freeze-dried raspberries

Using a small food processor, pulse the black sesame seeds until a fine, sandy powder forms. Add the freeze-dried raspberries and pulse until incorporated. Store in an airtight container in the freezer for up to 1 month.

Tray of Togetherness: Lucky Snacks for a Bountiful Finish

IF YOU'VE EVER rustled up dinner by combing through your fridge to build an impromptu snack plate, then this is the zero-stress hot pot finish for you. Tray of Togetherness is the traditional Chinese name given to the assortment of seeds, nuts, dried fruits, and candies that are arranged in a decorative lacquered red box during the Lunar New Year.

The treats symbolize various Chinese virtues and values (centering mostly on health, wealth, and family), and consumption of them throughout the two weeks of celebration is a strong way to begin the new year. The Tray of Togetherness can have compartments for six, eight, or nine different treats—all lucky numbers, of course.

Arrange the treats in small clusters on a large platter, cutting board, or in a partitioned box. Small bowls or cupcake liners can be used to compartmentalize the treats, but they're not necessary. Look for a mixture of textures, flavors, and colors, aiming for at least a small handful of each item for a group of four diners.

DRIED OR CANDIED FRUITS

- ☐ Apricots
- ☐ Banana chips
- ☐ Citrus peel
- ☐ Dates
- ☐ Jujubes
- ☐ Papaya
- ☐ Persimmons
- ☐ Pineapple spears
- ☐ Winter melon strips

ROASTED OR CANDIED NUTS AND SEEDS

- ☐ Almonds
- ☐ Cashews
- ☐ Hazelnuts
- ☐ Lotus seeds
- ☐ Melon seeds
- ☐ Nuts in their shell (look for walnuts, pecans, and pistachios)
- ☐ Peanuts, roasted and in their shell
- ☐ Pumpkin seeds

CANDY

- ☐ Candied ginger
- ☐ Chocolate coins or individual Rolos (or any candy symbolizing money or gold)
- ☐ Ferrero Rocher
- ☐ Fruit jellies (usually in flavors like white peach, muscat grape, and honeydew melon)
- ☐ Haw flakes (sour wafers made with hawthorn fruit)
- ☐ Sesame brittle
- ☐ White Rabbit (a milky, chewy candy with an edible rice wrapper)

DEALER'S CHOICE

- ☐ Granola bark
- ☐ Leaf-attached mandarins
- ☐ Mini marshmallows
- ☐ Toasted coconut flakes
- ☐ Whole kumquats

山楂餅
CHAN PUI MUI
LYCHEE GUMMY CANDY

Rainbow Tanghulu

MAKES 12 SKEWERS, OR 4 TO 6 SERVINGS

2 tangerines, peeled

1 lemon, peeled

1 cup (180 g) bite-size fruit, such as pineapple chunks, blueberries, or strawberries

4 cups (800 g) sugar

2 cups (480 ml) filtered water

HOT (POT) TIP

If you're new to making tanghulu, try starting with beginner skewers: just 1 piece of fruit per skewer, which makes them easier to dip and fully submerge in syrup. Picking the perfect pot is crucial, too—a 4-inch (10 cm) wide, ½-quart (473 ml) capacity sauce pot is ideal for this amount of syrup.

Tanghulu, a colorful snack of fresh fruits coated in a glassy rock sugar shell, dates from as far back as the Song dynasty, over a thousand years ago. Like most handheld food served on a stick or skewer, tanghulu is more of a street food, meant to be enjoyed while you're on the go, juices streaming down your chin. One bite quickly explains its enduring appeal: The crisp, clear casing of sugar, which works to both preserve and showcase the fresh fruit within, shatters with a satisfying crunch, giving way to a volcanically juicy bite. It's a dessert with a twist ending—a water balloon posing as a candied apple—and a little theater to cap a long hot pot feast.

You can dip the fruit skewers several hours in advance—you certainly shouldn't handle 300°F (149°C) syrup after a shot or three of baijiu—and the shells will stay crisp. For best results, you'll need a candy thermometer, which will guarantee the syrup is heated to a high enough temperature, thus preventing the dreaded stick-in-your-molars chew.

In North China, where tanghulu originated, the round, hard hawthorn fruit—imagine a plummy blend of apple and strawberries—is the most common ingredient used. While you could technically candy nearly any fruit with this syrup-dipping technique, for the most balanced (and least cloying) bite, choose only a naturally tart fruit, like the ones listed here, or dragon fruit, apples, nectarines, blackberries, or even cherry tomatoes. For sweeter fruits like melon, grapes, papaya, mango, kiwi, or banana, a small pinch of citric acid, sprinkled over the sugar shell before it fully hardens, brings balance.

PAIR IT WITH:
The Perfect Skewer
(page 39)

Line a baking sheet with parchment paper and set aside.

Split the peeled tangerines into quarters or individual segments, depending on the size. Separate the lemon into individual segments.

→

HOT (POT) TIPS

You *can* make tanghulu without a thermometer! While the syrup is boiling, place 3 spoons in the freezer. After 20 minutes, dip 1 spoon into the syrup; when you pull it out, the syrup coating the spoon should harden immediately and not appear sticky or drippy. Keep testing with the remaining spoons until the syrup achieves the proper glasslike set.

If the sugar shells get sticky or chewy, fill a pitcher with ice water and dunk in the skewers. The shells will magically re-crisp.

To efficiently clean your sugar-hardened tools, fill the dirty pot with water and bring to a simmer over high heat. The crust of sugar will loosen, making washing the pot a breeze.

Using bamboo skewers at least 6 inches (15 cm) long, thread the fruits through their centers, packing them tightly together on one end, about 2 to 3 one-inch-long (2.5 cm) fruits per skewer. Leave at least 3 inches (7.5 cm) of the skewer bare. Continue until all the fruits have been threaded onto skewers; you should have about 12 skewers.

Combine the sugar with the water in a small pot with deep sides and bring to a boil over medium-high heat. Swirl the pot occasionally (there's no need to whisk or stir), checking the temperature of the syrup until it reaches 300°F (149°C), 20 to 25 minutes.

When the syrup reaches 300°F (149°C), or the "hard crack" stage, reduce the heat to very low, and carefully tilt the pot toward you, then lower in one skewer, rolling it around in the syrup until the fruit is fully coated. Briefly hold the skewer over the pot, letting the excess syrup drip off, then transfer the skewer to the lined baking sheet. Repeat with the remaining skewers until they are all coated, working as quickly as you can while the syrup is at temperature.

In a cool kitchen, the shell will firm in a matter of minutes. Once set, store the skewers at room temperature, ideally in a cool, dry place, until you're ready to eat them.

Boba Rice Treats

MAKES TWENTY 2-INCH (5 CM) TREATS

1 cup (about 170 g) parcooked tapioca pearls

8 tablespoons (1 stick/110 g) unsalted butter

6 cups (about 10 ounces/280 g) mini marshmallows

2 teaspoons instant coffee

2 teaspoons white miso paste

1 teaspoon vanilla extract

6 cups (180 g) puffed rice cereal

PAIR IT WITH:
Bouquet Tea (page 198)

Tapioca pearls—a chewy, bouncy starch extracted from cassava root—are a hugely popular base ingredient for not-too-sweet desserts and refreshing drinks all over Asia, like Chinese dessert soups and Taiwanese bubble milk tea. In hot pot restaurants, it's one of the most popular ways to wrap up the meal, either sucked up through towering iced drinks or spooned over a mountain of shaved ice and condensed milk.

Here boba adds its addictive, elastic chewiness—an elusive texture known as "QQ" in Taiwan, where it's present in everything from bouncy noodles to jellies to fish cakes—to a classic bake sale staple: the Rice Krispies treat. These little pearls are a genius textural addition to a treat loaded with deeply umami flavors like brown butter, miso paste, and instant coffee. In an Asian grocery store, look for the parcooked tapioca pearls, right next to the instant coffee crystals. They'll blanch to a perfectly bouncy tenderness in just a few minutes.

Line a 9 by 5-inch (23 by 13 cm) loaf pan with a saddle of parchment paper, secure with tape, and set aside.

Fill a small bowl with ice cubes and water and set aside.

Bring a sauce pot of water to a boil. Add the tapioca pearls all at once, swirling them briefly to separate, and reduce the heat to a gentle simmer. The pearls will gradually rise to the surface as they soften, 3 to 4 minutes. (Always check the package instructions to account for varying cooking times.) Sample one before draining; they should be chewy and soft but not mushy.

Transfer the cooked tapioca pearls to the ice bath to halt cooking. Drain the pearls in a fine-mesh sieve and spread them out into one layer on a small tray. Place into the refrigerator to air-dry, at least 1 hour.

→

Melt the butter in a small pot over medium heat. After 2 to 3 minutes, the butter will heavily foam and bubble. As the milk solids settle to the bottom of the pot, the foam will burn off. Once the milk solids are golden brown, another 2 minutes, and the air smells nutty and sweet, add 5 cups (230 g) of the marshmallows, along with the instant coffee, white miso paste, and vanilla. Stir gently with a spatula until the marshmallows have melted and the mixture is glossy, thick, and emulsified, about 3 minutes.

Turn off the heat and add the dried tapioca pearls, stirring until they are thoroughly coated. Add the rice cereal to the pot, and fold gently to coat the cereal evenly.

Finally, add the remaining 1 cup (50 g) marshmallows, and fold gently to incorporate into the mixture.

Scrape the mixture into the prepared loaf pan and press down with your fingertips or a spatula to compact and smooth the surface.

Let cool at room temperature until firm, about 30 minutes.

Invert the loaf pan onto a large cutting board. Peel back the parchment paper and discard. Slice the loaf into five 2-inch-thick (5 cm) slabs, then slice each piece in half, then in half again, to yield 20 bite-size cubes. Eat immediately or within a few hours; the treats will lose some crispness as they rest.

Steamed Jujubes with Soy Sauce Caramel

SERVES 4

1 tablespoon honey

1 tablespoon dark brown sugar

1 tablespoon unsalted butter

1 tablespoon unsweetened coconut milk

2 teaspoons soy sauce

12 dried jujubes

2 tablespoons roasted soy nuts

HOT (POT) TIP Don't own a steaming rack? Create a DIY steam bath by inverting a small cake pan and fitting inside a larger braiser or stockpot. Scatter the dates on top of the elevated inverted pan and carefully pour the water into the surrounding moat.

PAIR IT WITH: *Tray of Togetherness (page 174), The Perfect Fruit Plate (page 184)*

Though commonly associated with the savory flavors of hot pot, jujubes, or red dates, are an endlessly versatile ingredient with many nutritive benefits. This antioxidant-rich superfood is native to South Asia and, once softened, has a taffy-like texture and a rich brown sugar flavor. Boiled with water and other superfood fruits like goji berries, jujubes make a popular postpartum tonic tea, replenishing and nourishing the body.

But it's also delicious in desserts, especially if you like things not too sweet. Because jujubes aren't as intense as date varieties like Medjool and Barhi, the addition of a sweet-and-salty caramel sauce spiked with soy sauce is a welcome garnish.

To make the soy sauce caramel, place the honey in a small pot and cook over medium heat until foaming and bubbly, just a minute or two. Add the brown sugar and butter and whisk until smooth. Add the coconut milk and let the mixture simmer for another minute. Remove from the heat and add the soy sauce. Stir and let cool at room temperature until you're ready to use it.

To steam the jujubes, fill a Dutch oven or medium pot with 1 inch (2.5 cm) of water and set a steaming rack snugly inside. Bring the water up to a bare simmer, then spread the jujubes onto the steaming rack and cover. Let them steam until soft, sticky, and fragrant, 6 to 8 minutes.

Using a small knife, slice the jujubes open lengthwise, pulling out the pits with your fingertips. Spread the jujube halves open, like the wings of a butterfly, and fill with the roasted soy nuts.

Spoon the soy sauce caramel on top. These are best enjoyed immediately.

The Perfect Fruit Plate: Health Is Wealth

BAKING ELABORATE, SWEET desserts is simply not a big thing in most Chinese households. In my family, we always left the sugar-and-cream wizardry to bakeries, cafes, and grocery stores, because we were a house ruled by fruit. If I hosted a playdate or my parents had colleagues over for tea, you could be sure that the gathering would end with a plate of fruit. Quartered apples, coins of banana, peeled tangerines, a handful of dates or blueberries—my mother would scrub, peel, and portion the fruit so that we, her loved ones, would not labor to enjoy it. Fruit is its own love language.

Fruit plays a highly symbolic role in Chinese restaurants, too, where the barest slip of cooling, fresh fruit is all that is needed to punctuate a hot meal of any kind. Unlike my mom's simple fruit plates, at banquet-style Chinese restaurants, the fruit plate can embody a seductive, artful, opulence, from sky-high fruit carvings to platters of ten exotic fruits or more. Final flourishes like edible flowers, blinking LED lights, and pebbled ice add to the atmosphere.

Where I live now in Brooklyn, I've had outstanding fruit plates at a laid-back Cantonese-American restaurant called Bonnie's, owned by the chef Calvin Eng. The porcelain plate is bursting with fruit, yet there is a sculptural order and graceful movement to the clusters of grapes, peeled kiwis and rambutan, shimmering orbs of citrus, and juicy slabs of jackfruit. Tristan Kwong, a Queens-born, first-generation Chinese American who goes by the nickname "Fruit Sommelier," a cheeky nod to his meticulous sourcing and precise knife cuts, helped shape those Bonnie's plates into the works of art that they are.

To guide you to a winning fruit plate, here are Tristan's best fruit plate practices.

There is a certain architecture. Treat the fruit plate like a fluid puzzle, moving pieces around until it looks just right. Tristan advises starting with the larger pieces first—like long wedges of melon or spears of mango—and then filling in the negative space with smaller clustered fruits, like lychee and rambutan.

Make it easy to eat. Fruit doesn't have to be bite-size, but your guests should experience some ease of eating. Tristan says you want to break down the fruits enough that someone else can easily interact with them. Watermelons can be cut into handheld slices, the rind pared down to just a little handle; lychees, longans, and tangerines can be peeled halfway, which allows a diner to pick up the fruit without getting their fingers sticky.

Aim for variety—or none at all. For thematic impact, try building a fruit plate around a single theme—like only spherical shapes, only red fruits, or only citrus varieties. Or aim to integrate as many fresh fruits as possible, with a mix of everything from common Western fruits (like strawberries, oranges, and apples) to tropical varieties (like dragon fruit, mango, and guava) to iconic Chinese fruits (like grapes, donut peach, plum, and pear).

Avoid frozen or canned, if you can. The fruit plate is about celebrating the excellence of fresh fruit. If you like, Tristan suggests a sprinkling of dried fruits, like raisins and dates.

Be ready to pivot. Choose the best looking and most fragrant fruits you can find. It's easier to find tangerines with leaf and stem attached in the winter, while juicy melons of all types appear in the markets during the summer.

This Heat

In southwestern China's Sichuan province, the hot pot feast is a mouth-numbing affair. Unlike the more tranquil broths found in the north (see page 67), here the hot pot base is dyed a brilliant vermillion, often fortified with a generous amount of beef tallow or chicken fat, and carpeted with a sea of bobbing dried chiles.

For Westerners, this soup is perhaps the most iconic and recognizable of all the hot pot variants, and it has a destabilizing, unforgettable effect on the senses, thanks to the Sichuan peppercorn. Known in Chinese as hua jiao—literally, "flower pepper"—the greenish red peppercorn contains a unique compound that, upon consumption, triggers a numbing, tingling sensation in the face that then feverishly floods the body.

The culinary philosophy of mala, one of the tentpoles of Sichuan cuisine, is a combination of two Chinese characters—*ma*, or numbing, referring to the prickly peppercorn, plus *la*, meaning spicy, for the chiles. After a long Sichuan hot pot, it's not uncommon to wobble out of the room slightly delirious, sporting a fine layer of sweat and flushed, rosy cheeks. Call it the mala effect, but there's something addictive about the combination of chiles and peppercorns that relaxes the body, banishes stress, and invites deep relaxation and contentment.

GET READY

Up to 2 weeks in advance, make the contrasting broths, one spicy and rich (Tingly Beef Broth, page 59) and one aromatic and cooling (Royal Chrysanthemum Broth, page 57). Sauces that improve with time can also be made in advance, so mix up the Cashew-Lime Salsa Macha (page 124) and the Charred and Candied Orange Sauce (page 121) up to 1 week in advance.

The day before, shape the Scallop and Fish Roe Dumplings (page 96), freezing them until you're ready to eat. Then mix the Black and White Shaobing (page 79), which can also be frozen, fully shaped, up to 2 weeks in advance.

Finally, run through your equipment checklist and visit the grocery store or farmers' market for any key missing ingredients.

HOT (POT) TIP

For an instant tableside marinade, place a small dish of grated garlic and chopped scallions topped with fancy toasted sesame oil near your hot pot ingredients. Dredge an uncooked morsel—like a slip of pork belly or sliced fish—in the dish, before swishing it around in the broth to cook it to tender, unctuous perfection.

The day of the party, prep and plate all the hot pot ingredients, and mix a batch of Al's Baijiu Punch (page 211). Juice and scrape the Honey Tangerine Granita (page 169) in the afternoon, though if you want a do-ahead you could mix the syrup base up to 2 days in advance and then freeze the morning of the party.

An hour before guests arrive, mix the Spicy Wood Ear Mushrooms (page 155), so the ingredients have time to mingle and marry. While guests are settling in, bake the shaobing, which will make your home smell wonderful and yeasty.

THE TABLESIDE STRATEGY

This feast can be challenging for those wary of mala: A slurp from the broth leaves a rosy, flaming ring of grease that coats your lips and tongue, while absorbent vegetables, noodles, and meats suck up the fiery liquid like a sponge. For this feast, the dual-chambered hot pot is strategic, as it makes room for both a spicy broth and a more sedate one, providing excitement and relief in equal measure. Advise your guests to take plenty of breaks from the tingly broth, using the Royal Chrysanthemum broth as a tool for reprieve.

THE MENU

EQUIPMENT LIST (see page 18)

KNIFE CUTS AND COOKING INSTRUCTIONS (see page 27)

RUN OF SHOW (see page 40)

THE BROTHS

2 quarts (1.9 L) Tingly Beef Broth (page 59)

2 quarts (1.9 L) Royal Chrysanthemum Broth (page 57)

THE SAUCES

1½ cups (400 g) Cashew-Lime Salsa Macha (page 124)

1½ cups (420 g) Charred and Candied Orange Sauce (page 121)

HOT (POT) TIP

Taiwanese-born chef Jessie Yu-Chen (bottom left) taught me a great trick: When a broth is extra oily, she'll remove some of the fat by filling a large soup ladle with ice cubes, waiting a minute, then dunking it into the boiling broth. The temperature shock immediately solidifies the fat, leaving it clinging to the ladle—and not in your soup.

THE DRINK

Al's Baijiu Punch (page 211)

THE DESSERT

Honey Tangerine Granita (page 169)

THE SPREAD

8 ounces (230 g) sliced pork belly

8 ounces (230 g) cubed fish fillet (like cod, haddock, sea bass, or halibut)

8 ounces (230 g) shrimp, peeled, with tails attached

4 ounces (115 g) fried tofu puffs

1 napa cabbage or similar (choose from The Hot Pot Ingredient Guide, page 30)

4 ounces (115 g) kabocha squash, thinly sliced

4 ounces (115 g) lotus root, sliced

4 ounces (115 g) daikon radish, cubed

2 ounces (55 g) king trumpet mushrooms, sliced into thin slabs

2 ounces (55 g) enoki mushrooms, torn into bite-size pieces

1 bunch fresh scallions, sliced

1 bunch cilantro, chopped

1 bunch watercress or similar (choose from The Hot Pot Ingredient Guide, page 28)

1 bunch dark, leafy greens (choose from The Hot Pot Ingredient Guide, page 29)

Discovering Hot Pot Theater: A Reflection

BY PAUL PICKOWICZ

THE FIRST TIME I was invited to a hot pot gathering in China back in the 1970s, I was struck by all the deeply meaningful rituals associated with hot pot culture. Seating, for example, was not random. The guest of honor was placed in the chair facing south or toward an open door because such a gesture conveys respect. I also learned that a round table was highly desirable because its harmonious and communal circularity allowed everyone to see and hear everyone else.

I noticed right away the eye-opening amount of food placed on the table. How could we eat that much food? It was as if the host was required to put out much more food than the guests could possibly consume. This, too, was a crucial aspect of hot pot rituals. A dramatic table display was auspicious. It spoke to abundance and celebration. The many leftovers meant that the host was doing well and could afford such a surplus.

It wasn't just the amount of food; it was also about an artistic set design—splendid displays that looked like art. Hosts clearly wanted their guests to think, "Wow! How lucky I am to be here!" Newcomers to hot pot were told that the decorative, stringy noodles that blessed the table represented a long life, and that the Chinese word for fish, *yu*, sounded like the word for prosperity.

The old-fashioned copper hot pot I acquired in China in 1978 was itself a work of art, a gorgeous theatrical prop. It is beautifully decorated with four stunning dragons ready to ward off evil spirits and protect all honored guests. It is also decorated with cascading, wavelike symbols of good health as well as eye-catching circular designs that look like ancient coins.

Once the hot pot stage was properly set, it was time for the members of the "audience" to become "players." It was time to eat! Continuing to talk to my hosts while keeping an eye on my submerged morsels was quite a challenge. Indeed, the very act of cooking was theatrical and competitive. The food in many individual scoops sometimes fell out and disappeared into the broth. You might find your missing food while still engaging in table talk, but someone else might grab it first!

There was another unforgettable component of hot pot theater, one that really caught me by surprise and had nothing to do with the food: A secret objective of the host was to get all guests to drink plenty of powerful sorghum whiskey (better known as baijiu or white lightning) served in small shot glasses. Early in the evening, the host stood and proposed a toast to the well-being of honored guests. How was it possible to say no? It was just a small shot. But then guests themselves were encouraged to rise up and make additional toasts. How was it possible to decline such culturally meaningful expectations? So I stood to make a toast. One by one the other guests got up to offer a few words, much to the delight of the main host—someone I began to think of as the "director" of the evening's hot pot production. The baijiu ritual was often repeated six or seven times in one evening.

I still cherish those early hot pot experiences. Yes, we all had way too much to eat and drink. But now, I'm the one to stand up to make the first of many toasts.

Hot Pot Through the Decades (*clockwise from far left*): *Our beloved bronze hot pot, 50 years old and handmade; from a recent trip to China, an old-school charcoal-burning stove; enjoying hot pot in Beijing in 1983, complete with a bottle of baijiu; using our favorite hot pot to host friends at home in the late 1980s.*

DRINKS

Staying Hydrated

Beverages are a key component of the hot pot table, a supporting actor happy to share the spotlight. Some drinks keep you hydrated, providing sustaining energy, while others soothe the palate, offering creamy or refreshing relief after never-ending spicy bites. Some drinks are ritualistic, to punctuate the meal with long speeches and grandstanding. Some are flamboyant, adding even more visual drama to an already packed table. And some can be potent, delivering a boozy hit to the senses, stoking the appetite for even more trips to the hot pot.

In many of my favorite all-you-can-eat hot pot restaurants, large reach-in refrigerators offer a variety of nonalcoholic drinks that can be enjoyed with no limits—fizzy seltzers spiked with pineapple, cold cans of Coke and Sprite, foil-capped soy milk in tiny plastic jugs. Other drinks, ordered à la carte, are more ornate and shareable: huge carafes of freshly squeezed watermelon juice, iced hawthorn tea, or salted plum juice; pitchers of soju, a Korean rice liquor, garnished with melon balls and flowers; mini kegs of Asian beers; massive coconuts hacked open tableside; frothy lychee and dragon fruit smoothies; Hong Kong–style milk tea; and tumblers of hot, creamy corn juice. At home, beverages of this nature can easily be made from scratch, from the Watermelon Shiso Slushies (page 205) to the Hawthorn Berry Shrub (page 201)—drinks for refreshment and reprieve.

In general, the themes of abundance and variety carry over into your beverage offerings. In addition to hot tea and water, offer cold beers for the cold beer drinkers (try easy-drinking lagers like Sapporo or Harbin) and chilled wines for the chilled wine drinkers, and, of course, keep a bottle of baijiu or Hennessy, both beloved by Chinese drinkers of all ages and proclivities, waiting in the wings.

Bouquet Tea

SERVES 4

1 quart (950 ml) filtered water

One 1-inch (2.5 cm) piece ginger, sliced thinly

1 tablespoon dried chrysanthemum

1 tablespoon dried roselle

1 tablespoon dried chamomile

1 tablespoon dried rosebuds

If you're Chinese, tea isn't just a beverage; it's a lifestyle. In many restaurants, a pot of sturdy, utilitarian tea—which opens up the palate and prepares the stomach for the incoming meal—is more common on the table than tap water. Finishing a meal with a smoother, more mellow herbal tea can help with digestion and feelings of satiety.

Many Asian grocery stores sell loose herbal teas in large, more affordable quantities, making it easier than ever to brew your own bespoke blend. Look for whole dried flowers (rather than a finely ground tea), similar to what you'd use for a tisane, which allows the full beauty of the blossom to express itself.

Pour the water into a medium pot set over high heat and bring it just up to steaming. Add the ginger slices and dried flowers, cover, and let steep for 5 minutes. Strain through a fine-mesh sieve, then serve. (The dried flowers and ginger can be reused for up to two additional changes of water.)

HOT (POT) TIPS

Noncaffeinated floral teas are delicious cold; strain the tea after steeping, let cool to room temperature, then pour into a glass over ice.

Build your own bouquet: Butterfly pea flower, white peony, lemongrass, calendula, and mint would all be delicious substitutes.

PAIR IT WITH:
Tea Bag Broth (page 53)

Kasugai
Kiss
Candy

Hawthorn Berry Shrub

SERVES 4

1 ounce (30 g) dried hawthorn berries (see Resources, page 214)

2 cups (480 ml) filtered water

¼ cup (50 g) sugar

¼ cup (60 ml) apple cider vinegar

Ice cubes

One 12-ounce (355 ml) can plain seltzer or club soda

2 tablespoons cubed fruit, such as dragon fruit or honeydew melon (optional)

PAIR IT WITH:
Garden Wontons (page 101), Crunchy Seaweed Boats (page 152)

Hawthorn berry, or haw fruit, is a small, hard fruit native to China, with a uniquely sweet-and-sour flavor, like strawberries, plums, cherries, and apples all jumbled together. As a kid, my favorite candy was haw flakes, a stout paper-wrapped tube containing thin, quarter-sized disks that melt on your tongue. You're just as likely to see hawthorn used for medicinal purposes—the little fruits pack a huge amount of antioxidants—but I love its culinary potential, cooking it into jellies, teas, candies, ice pops, and, most traditionally, tanghulu (see page 177).

Here you'll make a vivid syrup, using dried hawthorn berries and a little bit of sugar, to form the base of your shrub, which is a kind of soft drink that uses vinegar and fruit juices to add sourness and punch. It's a fabulous nonalcoholic option for those long hot pot nights—refreshing and lively and fizzy all at once.

Combine the dried hawthorn berries, water, and sugar in a small pot over high heat. Bring to a boil, then reduce the heat to low and simmer until the full flavor of the berries is extracted and the liquid is reduced by half, about 30 minutes. Remove from the heat and let cool completely, then strain. Stir in the apple cider vinegar. (The leftover spent berries can be tossed into a hot pot broth, page 32.)

When you're ready to serve, fill four glasses with ice. Divide the hawthorn and vinegar syrup evenly among the glasses. Top with the seltzer. Add a skewer of cubed fruit to garnish, if desired. Drink immediately.

Salted Plum Lemonade

SERVES 4

2 cups (480 ml) freshly squeezed lemon juice (from about 12 to 15 large lemons)

½ cup (about 15 g) dried roselle or hibiscus

3 cups (720 ml) cold filtered water

Salted Plum Syrup (recipe follows)

Ice cubes

Just like chugging down a fluorescent, sodium-rich energy drink after a long night of drinking, this salty-sweet lemonade is both delicious *and* strategic in preventing dehydration. Dried salted plums, or huamei, are a popular traditional ingredient in Chinese drinks, snacks, and sweets—and are incredibly yummy and complex-tasting to boot.

To make your own electrolyte-rich refreshment, simmer dried salted plums in sugar, then use this tangy syrup for creating a vibrant, vermillion punch. Don't forget the ratio for a just-sour-enough lemonade: two parts freshly squeezed lemon juice, two parts water, and one part syrup. This makes a big batch—everyone will want seconds of your new favorite hangover cure.

FIND IT IN:
The Endless Forest Feast (page 157)

Combine the lemon juice and roselles in a quart-sized jar or container. Let the mixture sit, chilled in the refrigerator, for about 30 minutes, or until the juice has turned a bright fuchsia hue.

Strain the mixture into a pitcher or container. Add the cold filtered water and Salted Plum Syrup and stir well. Pour over glasses filled with ice and drink immediately.

Salted Plum Syrup

MAKES 1 CUP (300 G)

1 cup (240 ml) filtered water

½ cup (100 g) sugar

½ cup (40 g) dried salted plums (see Resources, page 214)

Combine the water, sugar, and salted plums in a small pot. Bring to a simmer over medium-low heat, swirling the pot occasionally, until the syrup is slightly thickened and deeply yellow, about 15 minutes.

Remove from the heat and strain into a heatproof container. Let cool completely before using. (Nibble on the softened preserved plums as a snack, or discard.)

Watermelon Shiso Slushies

SERVES 4

3 pounds (1.4 kg) seedless watermelon, with the rind removed

1 cup (240 ml) filtered water

½ cup (100 g) sugar

10 purple shiso leaves, plus 4 more for garnish

Pinch of citric acid (optional)

1 cup (220 g) ice cubes

Juice of 1 lemon

HOT (POT) TIP If you can't find shiso at the grocery store, don't fret—torn mint leaves, perilla leaves, or lemon verbena are all delicious substitutes.

PAIR IT WITH: *Asian Pear, Jicama, and Fennel Slaw (page 145)*

Freshly squeezed watermelon juice is a staple at hot pot restaurants—it's just as refreshing as water, but obviously more delicious. For those long, sticky summer nights, there's no better pairing for hot pot than frosty watermelon slush, spiked with a sweet kiss of shiso. If you'd like to give it a boozy spin, tip an ounce of baijiu into each glass.

Cut the watermelon into chunks the size of ice cubes; you should have about 6 cups (1.4 kg) cubed watermelon. Spread them out on a baking sheet.

Transfer the baking sheet to the freezer and let the watermelon freeze completely, about 1 hour. Transfer the frozen cubed watermelon to an airtight container and keep in the freezer for up to 2 weeks.

To make shiso syrup, combine the water, sugar, and shiso leaves in a small pot. Bring to a simmer and continue to cook until the liquid has reduced by half and looks thick and sticky, about 15 minutes. Let cool completely. Add a pinch of citric acid, if desired, for a bit of tartness and to set the pink hue. Transfer to an airtight container and store in the refrigerator for up to 1 week.

When you're ready to make the slush, set four glasses in the freezer. Combine the frozen watermelon cubes, ice, and lemon juice in a blender (depending on the size of your blender, you may have to do this in two batches). Pulse the mixture until it catches on the blade, then puree on high speed until a thick slush forms.

Pull the glasses from the freezer. Pour 1 teaspoon of shiso syrup in the bottom of each glass, followed by ¼ cup (80 g) of slush. Repeat, alternating syrup and slush until the glasses are full. Garnish each glass with a shiso leaf and serve immediately.

Wine and Hot Pot: The More the Merrier

HOW DO YOU PAIR WINE with a feast that is inherently modular and theoretically infinite? What do you drink when each person's hot pot journey—from the personally customized sauces to a broth that literally transforms over the course of a few hours—looks a little different? To get a more authoritative perspective, I turned to Annie Shi, one of the most passionate wine professionals I know. Annie knows wine. As a first-generation Chinese American growing up in New York City, Annie brought her love of old-world, low-intervention wine to King, the Soho restaurant she opened in 2016 alongside the chefs Jess Shadbolt and Clare de Boer, and to Jupiter, their sister restaurant, just a few years later and now her natural wine bar Lei, in Manhattan's Chinatown.

The challenges with matching wine with Chinese food arises when you consider that so many meals are served family style—a dozen dishes or more of many different ingredients, textures, temperatures, and flavors.

Annie's solution? She sees these grand feasts as an opportunity to treat wine tasting as a communal, exploratory adventure. Just like hot pot itself, the act of experiencing wine can be casual, and interactive.

Whether you're providing the wine yourself or asking guests to bring a bottle, Annie shared some important points for selecting wines for your next hot pot feast.

What to avoid. Steer clear of tannic red wines, like Cabernet Sauvignon and Barolos, which are tough to pair with both the kind of spice present in dried chiles and peppercorns as well as gentler dishes that have a lot of umami. Also avoid heavily oaked wines; the butteriness is a tricky match for the numerous sauces present.

Instead, look for acid and texture. Try lighter-style reds, anything you might drink a little cooler, and textural whites with acidity—in other words, anything with skin contact, like wines from the Jura. Look for Savagnin, a signature Jura grape with a mouth-puckering acidity.

Vegetarian hot pot loves a dark rosé. Try versatile darker rosés or lighter reds, especially an Italian grape called Cerasuolo d'Abruzzo, a cherry-red rosé, for its versatility and freshness.

And you can't go wrong with all styles of white wine, especially skin-contact varieties, or wines with a bit of fizz or acidity. Look for any Vermentino or Pigato from Liguria (Annie loves the Punta Crena imported by Kermit Lynch), and from Provence an easy-to-find pét-nat (short for *pétillant naturel*, an old-world method of making naturally sparkling wine) like Super Modeste, from Domaine de Sulauze.

Think a little sweet. Chenin Blanc or Rieslings can vary from bone dry to dessert-wine sweet and everything in between. Look for Huet or Bellivière for off-dry Chenins. For off-dry German Rieslings, look for the words *Halbtrocken* (half dry) or *Feinherb* (a style falling between dry and off-dry) on the label.

If all else fails, bubbles are best. In many Chinese homes, hot pot is a celebratory meal held during important holidays, like the Lunar New Year. Now is the time to impress guests and elders with fancy bottles!

Baijiu Shooters

MAKES 10 SHOTS

1 ounce (30 g) demerara sugar or turbinado sugar

1 ounce (30 ml) filtered water

6 ounces (175 ml) baijiu, like Ming River (see Resources, page 214)

4½ ounces (130 ml) fresh lime juice (from about 6 limes)

Ice cubes

FIND IT IN:
The Northern Classic Feast (page 67)

Baijiu, with its tropical fruit overtones and innate sweetness, is the perfect swap for rum in a daiquiri, a classic cocktail that requires only three ingredients. At hot pot, your guests might find the endless shots of baijiu, served neat, too intense to drink all at once, let alone repeated many times. A batched cocktail, divided into shots, is a great way to make the spirit more approachable, while still allowing everyone to partake in the toasting and speech giving.

You'll mix the recipe, then store it in a glass bottle, which can be presented tableside, set into an ice bucket, alongside prechilled shot glasses. Don't forget to toast with the ceremonial *gan bei!*—a traditional Chinese incantation that literally translates to "make the cup dry"—tipping your now-empty glass to prove you drank it all.

Combine the sugar and water in a small saucepan over low heat. Bring to a simmer and cook for 3 to 4 minutes, until the syrup is slightly thickened and tawny in hue. Remove from the heat and let cool completely.

Meanwhile, place a large glass bottle in the freezer.

Fill a cocktail shaker with ice. Add the cooled syrup, baijiu, and lime juice. Shake well. Taste; the drink should be sweet and sour in equal measure.

Strain the liquid into the prechilled bottle. Serve immediately, or store in the freezer for up to 2 days.

When you're ready to drink, pour about 1½ ounces (45 ml) into each shot glass. Gan bei!

Al's Baijiu Punch

SERVES 4 TO 6

3 ounces (90 ml) baijiu

3 ounces (90 ml) Batavia arrack, preferably van Oosten brand

3 ounces (90 ml) Suze

3 ounces (90 ml) fresh lime juice

3 ounces (90 ml) yuzu juice (see Resources, page 214)

3 ounces (90 ml) Salted Parsley Syrup (recipe follows)

6 ounces (175 ml) brewed green tea, chilled

3 quarts (about 1.3 kg) ice cubes

Lime slices, for garnish

Edible flowers, for garnish

FIND IT IN:
This Heat Feast (page 187)

Though baijiu is traditionally consumed as a down-in-one shot, not everybody has the stamina (or desire!) to drink it on its own. I learned to make this punch from my friend Al Culliton, historian and bartender. You'll pair baijiu with Batavia arrack, a sugarcane and rice spirit produced in Indonesia, and layer in Suze, a French gentian liqueur with a bittersweet flavor and a grounding earthiness, along with lime juice, yuzu juice, a savory parsley syrup, and green tea. The drink is a brilliantly herbaceous, party-friendly punch, served from a communal bowl with a ladle—just like hot pot itself.

Combine the baijiu, arrack, Suze, lime juice, yuzu juice, Salted Parsley Syrup, and green tea in a nonreactive container. Allow to meld for 4 to 8 hours.

When you're ready to serve, carefully pour the mixture into a large punch bowl. Add the ice cubes. Garnish with lime slices and edible flowers. Serve in small glasses with a punch ladle.

Salted Parsley Syrup

MAKES 1¼ CUPS (ABOUT 450 g)

1 cup plus 2 tablespoons and 1 teaspoon (230 g) sugar

½ cup (120 ml) hot water

Ice cubes

Kosher salt

1 small bunch parsley (about 2½ ounces/75 g)

½ ounce (15 ml) vodka

Combine the sugar and hot water in a heatproof bowl or other container and stir until completely dissolved. If necessary, transfer to a saucepan over low heat and warm until just dissolved. Set aside; allow the syrup to cool completely.

Prepare a large bowl with equal parts water and ice. Bring a small pot of salted water to boil (salted like you're making pasta). Blanch the parsley in the boiling water for 15 seconds. Immediately submerge it in the prepared ice bath for 10 seconds. Pat dry with a towel.

→

Combine the parsley and simple syrup in a blender. Blend until the syrup turns green and the parsley is very finely chopped. Strain through a nut milk bag or a fine-mesh sieve, discarding the parsley pulp.

Mix in the vodka. Use immediately, or transfer to an airtight container and store in the refrigerator for up to 1 week.

Baijiu, an Impish Hot Pot Sidekick

BAIJIU, A CLEAR GRAIN ALCOHOL usually made with fermented sorghum, is the most infamous player at the hot pot table, and its close association with hot pot goes back hundreds of years. At a liquor store, a bottle can range from $50 to $5,000. It's easily the most popular spirit in China; higher-end classics like Moutai are a popular gift among businessmen or families, and newer brands like Ming River are proliferating on cocktail menus in trendy restaurants across the United States.

With its high alcohol content—a typical baijiu is usually 45 to 55 percent alcohol—this Chinese spirit has earned its nickname of "firewater," and it is still not fully appreciated by Western drinkers. The liquor has a unique capacity to dissolve feelings of fullness and works as a devilish, dizzying foil to a gut-busting hot pot spread. Baijiu has a bodily effect, too: Its consumption causes cheeks to flush, temples to sweat, and limbs to tingle. Though the spirit is clear, baijiu is anything but tasteless—just a sniff can summon a panoply of tropical fruits, like ripe pineapple, papaya, and guava; there's clear gummy bears, pink peppercorns, thick honey, ripe cheese, and honeydew melon, too. It is a delicious, naughty match for all the big, savory flavors of hot pot.

Resources

If you love shopping, you'll love hot pot. And if you *don't* love running to a bunch of different specialty shops, the beauty of the Asian grocery store is that it's often a one-stop-shop: You'll find everything from table settings to fresh produce to hard-to-find condiments to the hot pot stove itself. Even if you don't have one where you live, online retailers are indispensable resources, too; I like to bookmark my frequent stops to keep track of my favorites.

ASIAN SUPERMARKETS, SHOPS, AND SUPERETTES

Smaller Asian shops and convenience stores usually focus on the cuisine of a particular country, with an emphasis on prepared foods, snacks, and drinks. Larger supermarkets, on the other hand, often stock all kinds of useful things so you're not bound to one culinary tradition. Plus, they truly have it all, including bakeries with fresh bread, tricky-to-find dried mushrooms and teas, and vast seafood and butcher counters. One-of-a-kind indie shops, like Yun Hai in Brooklyn, New York, are even more curated: You might find everything from imported dried fruits to cookbooks to cute rice cookers. These are some of my tried-and-true favorites.

Supermarkets

NIJIYA MARKET
nijiya.com

MITSUWA MARKETPLACE
mitsuwa.com

99 RANCH
99ranch.com

SKYFOODS
skyfoods.com

J-MART
j-mart.us.com

GREAT WALL SUPERMARKET
gw-supermarket.com

H MART
Hmart.com

ZION MARKET
zionmarket.com

MARUKAI MARKET
marukai.com

Convenience stores, superettes, and specialty shops

SUNRISE MART
sunrisemart.com

KATAGIRI JAPANESE GROCERY
katagiri.com

MOGMOG
instagram.com/mogmog_lic

YUN HAI
yunhai.shop

MIDORIYA SUPERMARKET
instagram.com/midoriya_ny

HOME IMPROVEMENT RETAILERS AND HARDWARE STORES

For everything from portable camping stoves to gas to utilitarian furniture, your favorite hardware store likely has everything you need to get the fire started.

HOME DEPOT
homedepot.com

LOWE'S
lowes.com

ACE HARDWARE
acehardware.com

KITCHENWARE, TABLEWARE, AND DECOR

Half the fun of hot pot is getting the table to look just right. I source pieces from small shops that specialize in everything from artisanal heirloom pieces to more kitsch everyday offerings.

WING ON WO & CO.
wingonwoand.co

KORIN
korin.com

PEARL RIVER MART
pearlriver.com

MUSUBI KILN
musubikiln.com

CIBONE O'TE
cibone-us.com

TOIRO KITCHEN & SUPPLY
toirokitchen.com

JB PRINCE
jbprince.com

ALL-CLAD
all-clad.com

BONUS! Insider tips from a New York City stylist and artist

Here are some retail recommendations for setting a picture-perfect table from New York City–based prop stylist and artist Kalen Kaminski, who expertly mixes and matches unexpected pieces at all price points into celebratory, sophisticated, and animated tablescapes.

MELLOW
mellownyc.com

Artist Elise has her ceramics shop/studio on Allen Street in the Lower East Side. She makes the most beautiful bowls, plates, incense holders, and mugs. She also teaches workshops.

FREDERICKS & MAE
fredericksandmae.com

Here, Gabe and Gio sell everything from tabletop items to lighting to cool hardware gadgets. They design their own line of home goods and also sell other artisans' work.

UPSTATE STUDIO
youreupstate.com

My own brand is a small collection of textiles, glassware, and home goods. I make linens, bedding, glassware, lighting, and host workshops in my space.

SAM WARKOV
instagram.com/swarkov_

Sam makes beautiful beeswax candles of space-like creatures hugging and dancing. I use them at every dinner party and they're always a hit.

Acknowledgments

I'd like to extend my deepest gratitude to everyone who contributed to the creation of *Everyone Hot Pot*. It was an unbelievable privilege to research and write about a culinary tradition that has so thoroughly shaped who I am not just as a chef but as a person, a process made even richer by the quality of the collaborators that brought it to life.

I was very fortunate to work again with the brilliant minds at Artisan. My editor Judy Pray, who keeps things smooth and running while pushing and sculpting, you see how a book should be and then make it so. To my publisher Lia Ronnen—thank you for understanding that I am *More Than Cake*. To my art director Nina Simoneaux—I'm blown away by your mind. And to Brooke Beckmann, Moira Kerrigan, Theresa Collier, Alana Bonfiglio, Hillary Leary, and Donna Brown, thank you. To my indefatigable book agent Kitty Cowles, I'm so lucky to have you in my corner—thank you.

We shot the book during a sticky New York City heat wave, which was not exactly easy. Thank you to the artist and prop stylist Kalen Kaminski and her assistant Brenna Mahoney. Thank you to the food stylist/chef dream team of Tyna Hoang and Andrea Nguyen, for bringing your unparalleled experience (and reassurance and tool kit). Thank you to photographer Alex Lau—I knew back when this book was just a kernel of an idea that it could only be lensed by your eye.

Thank you to Annie Shi, Tristan Kwong, and Al Culliton for contributing your valuable insights from your respective fields—I'm so grateful for our exchange of knowledge, traditions, and ideas. Thank you to Honey's Brooklyn, Upstate Studio, and Sugar Studio, the locations around New York City where we shot the book.

Thank you to all the great people who gamely participated in the four feasts, infusing the images with the kinetic joy so crucial to hot pot: Jen Monroe, Steven Reker, Alison Leiby, Lindsey Peckham, Fred Winkler, Jessie Yu-Chen, Christina Chaey, Iris Tabarsky-Tasa, Adam Nguyen, and Todd Heim (who also designed the incredible bibs on page 118).

Thank you to the businesses that contributed to the making of this book, all places that I regularly shop from in my everyday life: Norwich Meadows Farm, Prospect Butcher Co., Natoora, Tivoli Mushrooms, Rosenthal Wine Merchant, Ming River Baijiu, Burlap & Barrel, Okamoto Studio, YUZUCO, Sophie Lou Jacobsen, Porto, and All-Clad Cookware. Thank you to Ivy Weinglass of IIIVVVYYY Ceramics and Danielle Chutinthranond of Monsoon Pottery for providing such beautiful pieces to showcase this food.

I also want to thank every single person who has joined me at the hot pot table, downed a shot, or slid a shrimp onto my plate, you know who you are. Thank you and I love you.

Thank you to everyone who helped me cross-test the recipes: Shirine Sajjadi, Maggie Helmick, Leanne Gan, Jessica Sbarsky, Anna Gill, Christine Foote, Elana Schulman, Ella Quittner, Bronwen Wyatt, Ida Rifkin, Salley Koo, Sophie Jenkins, Julia Buchmiller, Garrett Loh, Divya Jayachandran, and Nikki Metzgar.

On top of passing down their knowledge so I could inhabit the world of hot pot on my own, my parents were incredibly involved in the production of this book. My mom illustrated the book (our second together!), a task that she executed with her typical flair, humor, and dizzying, tremendous detail. And my dad, who provided critical, meticulous fact-checking throughout, also wrote a great essay just for this book. I was nervous about getting all of the details right, from my pinyin romanization to the historical timeline—but lucky for me, I happen to have one of the world's finest historians as a father, from whom I inherited a love of writing, research, and (because everything in balance) partying. Suffice to say I wouldn't be the person I am today without you guys—I really hope this book makes you proud. Thank you.

Index

Page numbers in *italics* refer to photos.

NATASHA PICKOWICZ is a California-born, New York City–based chef, a four-time James Beard Foundation Award finalist, and the author of *More Than Cake*, which was named a *New York Times* Best Cookbook of 2023 as well as a James Beard Foundation finalist in the baking category.

Natasha's recipes and writing have been published in *The New York Times*, *Vogue* magazine, *The Wall Street Journal*, *Bon Appétit*, *Saveur*, *Food & Wine*, *New York* magazine, and *Cherry Bombe*. Follow her on Instagram and Substack at @natashapickowicz.